Hope British Columbia and Area Canada in Colour Photos, Saving Our History One Photo at a Time

Photography
by Barbara Raué
©2018

Series Name:
Cruising Canada

Book 14: Hope B.C.

Cover photo: Nickel Plate Mountain, Hedley

© 2018 by Barbara Raue - All the photos in this book have been taken with my cameras. I own the rights to them.

Hope is located at the confluence of the Fraser and Coquihalla Rivers. Hope is at the eastern end of the Fraser Valley, and is at the southern end of the Fraser Canyon.

The history of European settlement in the town of Hope is linked with the history of the Hudson's Bay Company and the partnership between the company surveyors and First Nations in establishing a brigade trail through the mountains to Fort Kamloops. When gold was discovered in the Fraser Canyon in 1858, miners from across the continent flocked to British Columbia to seek their fortune in the mountains and creeks. Two years later gold was discovered in the Cariboo and miners migrated further north to seek riches in the area around Barkerville. In order to facilitate the movement of miners and supplies north, and gold south, the government built the Cariboo Wagon Road which allowed merchants and prospectors to travel faster and hopefully more safely.

The Fraser River has been the greatest source of food for the Sto-lo people who formed permanent settlements along the river. Simon Fraser came down the river in 1808. Hudson's Bay forts such as Hope (built in 1848-49) and Yale gave the Sto-lo access to a wider variety of trade goods, such as steel tools, cooking pots, and guns.

Keremeos is located in the beautiful Similkameen Valley in the Southern Interior of British Columbia. Keremeos' main industries are horticulture, agriculture, ranching, and wine making. Soft fruits such as apples, cherries, and peaches as well as vegetables are grown in the dry warm climate.

Princeton lies just east of the Cascade Mountains. The Tulameen and Similkameen Rivers converge here. The area's main industry has been mining of copper, gold, coal, and some platinum.

Gold was found on Nickel Plate Mountain in 1898 in Hedley. The ore was rich but it had to be extracted from the host rock by crushing and chemical treatment.

Hope

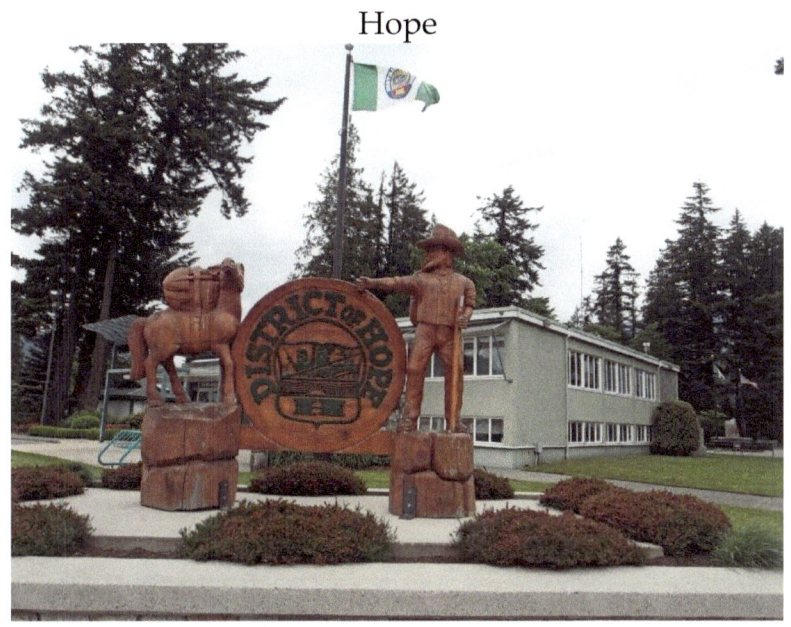

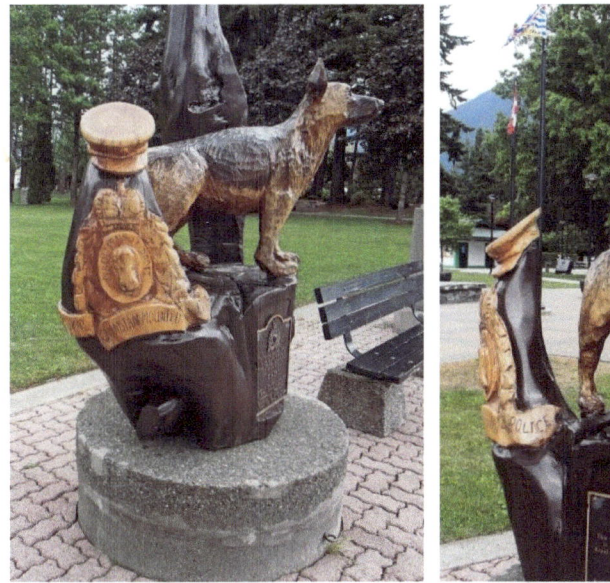
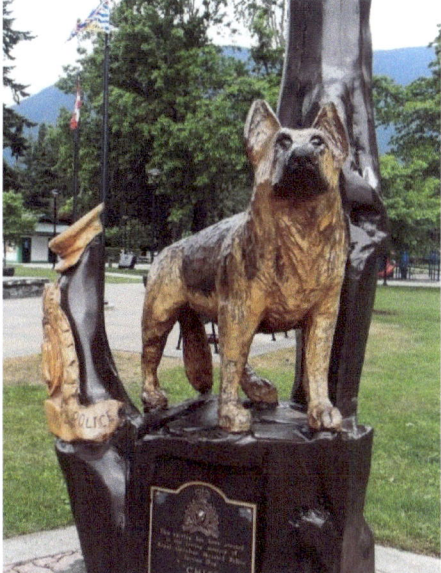

Royal Canadian Mounted Police Service Dog "Chip" was killed in the line of duty near Hope on September 13, 1996 while protecting his partner and friend Constable Doug Lewis.

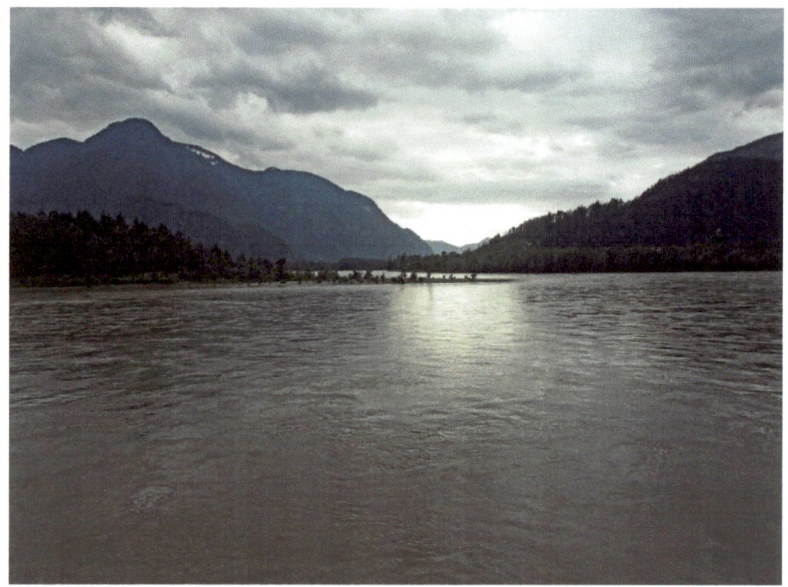

The past saw fur traders, the gold rush of 1858, and early settlers. The present sees waters teeming with migrating salmon and a highway and railways confined to the gorge carved by the river. The Fraser River, beautiful, bountiful, and powerful flows in the pattern of our future.

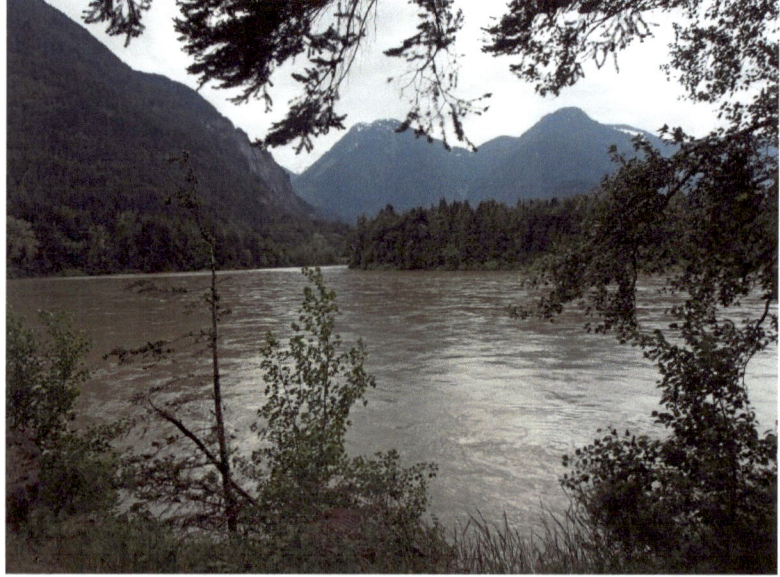

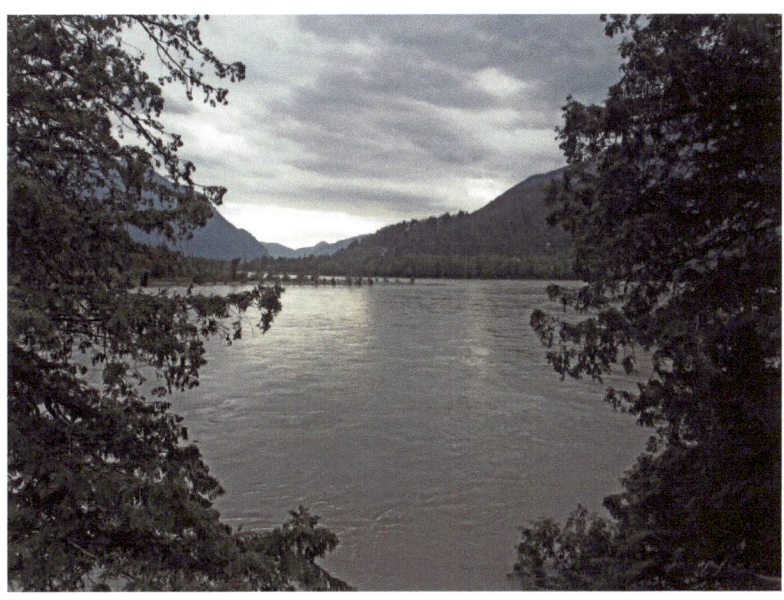

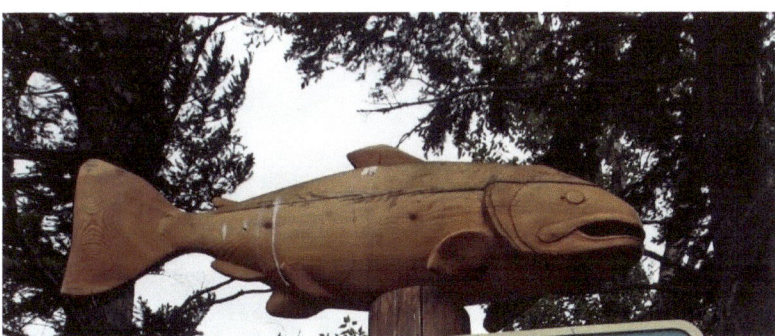

The first chainsaw carving appeared on Wallace Street in 1991. It was carved from a Douglas fir by Pete Ryan. Every two years the International Chainsaw Carving Competition comes to Hope.

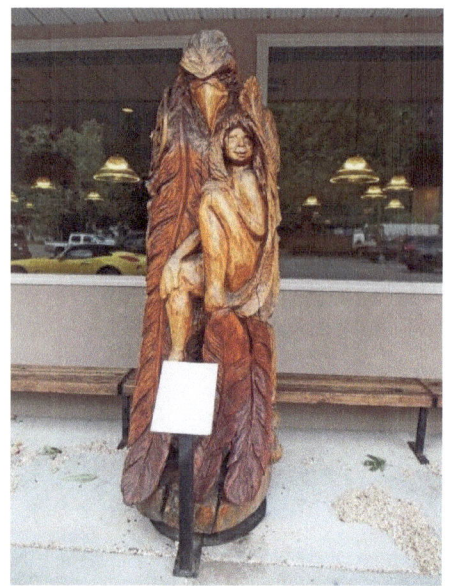
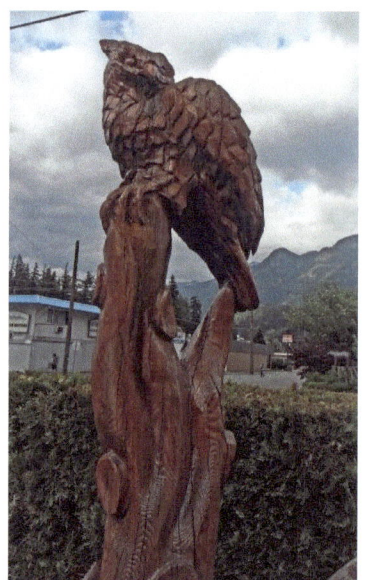

Making a Footprint in the Community
& Lives of the People of Hope
Carver: Angie Polyglaze

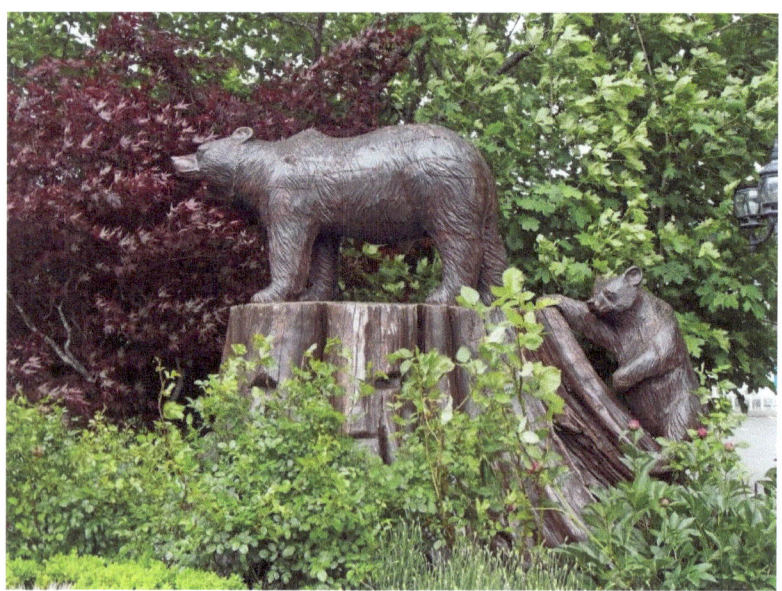

Two Bears

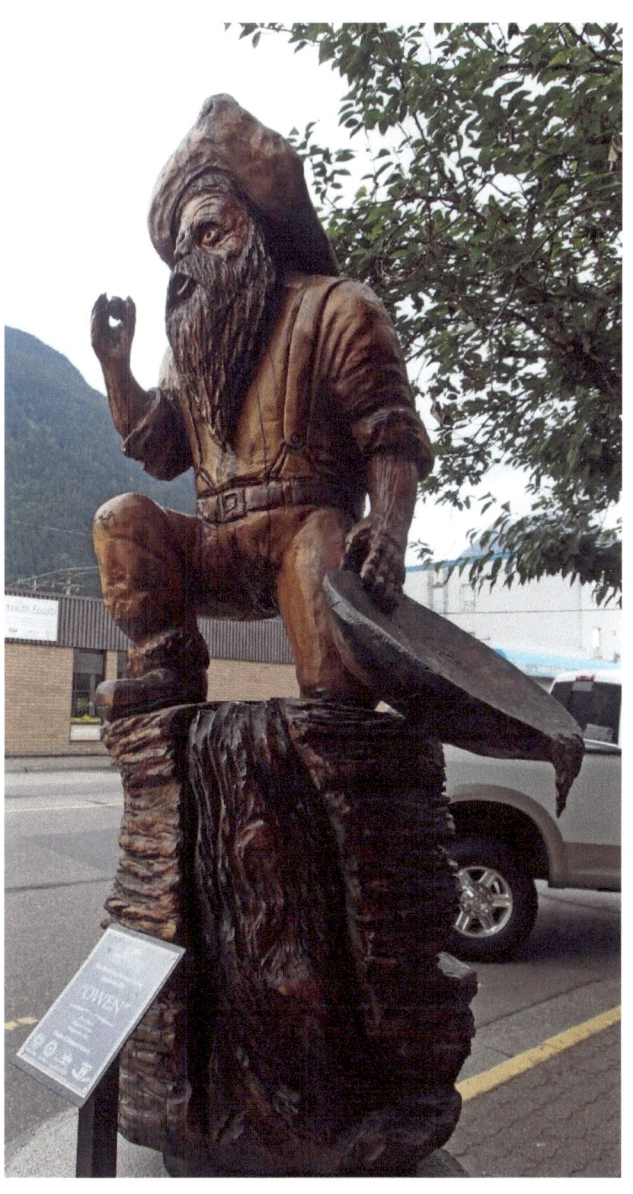

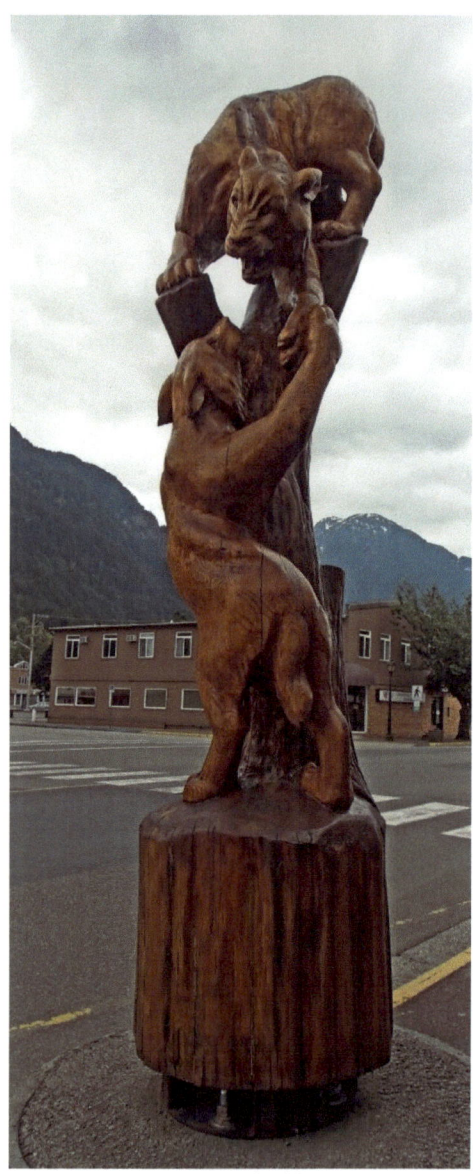

Standoff

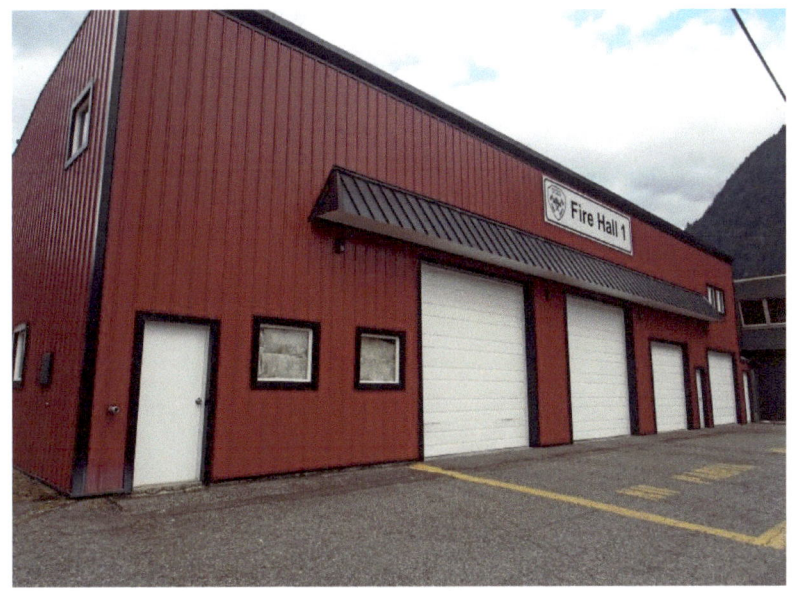
Fire Hall

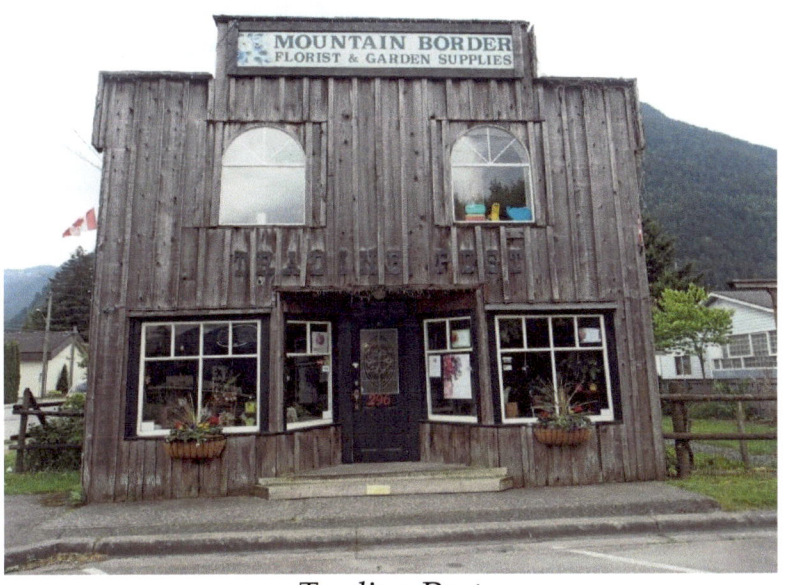
Trading Post

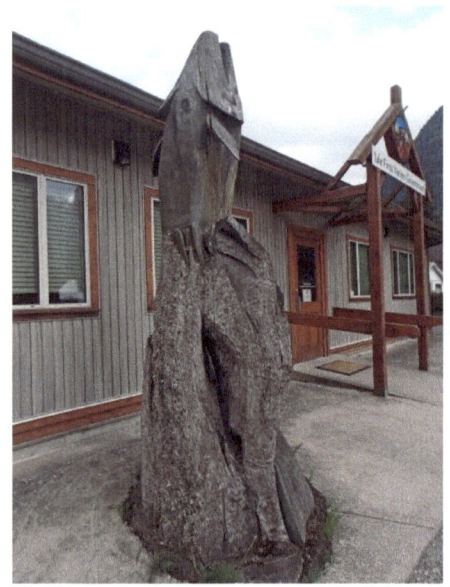
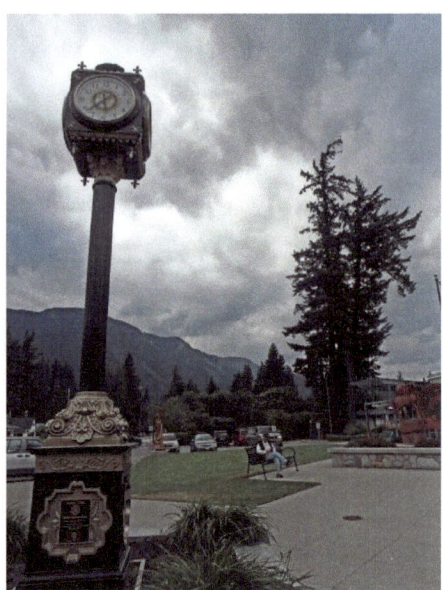

Fish

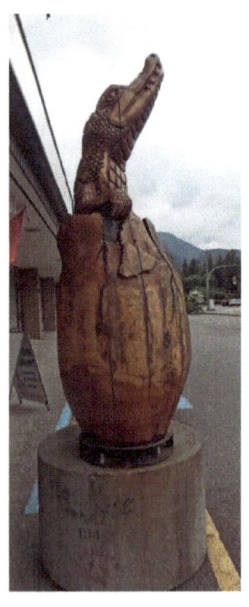
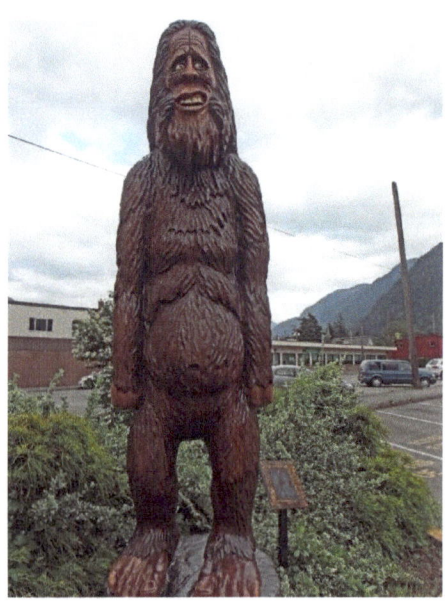

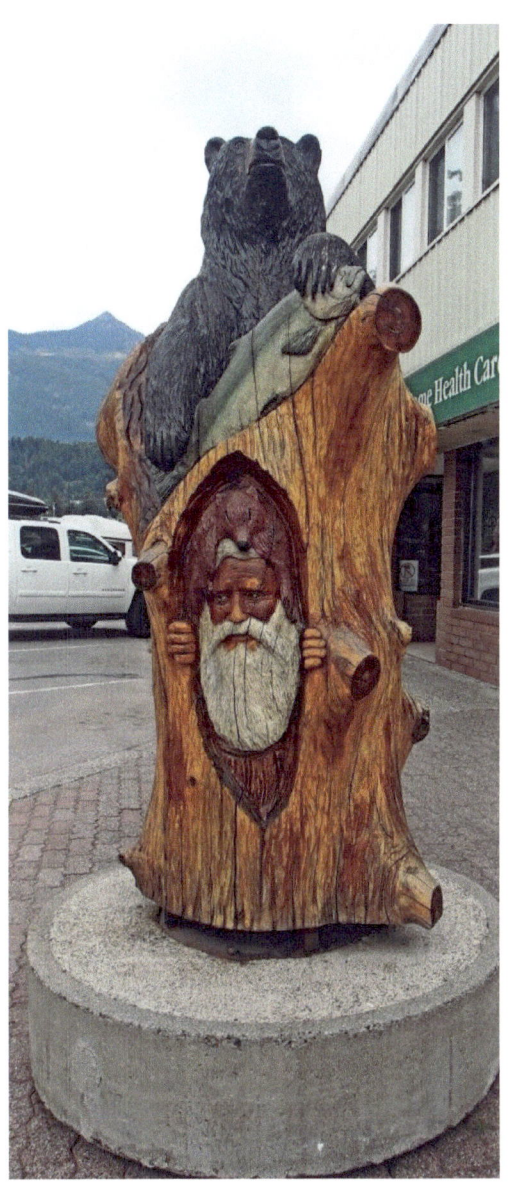

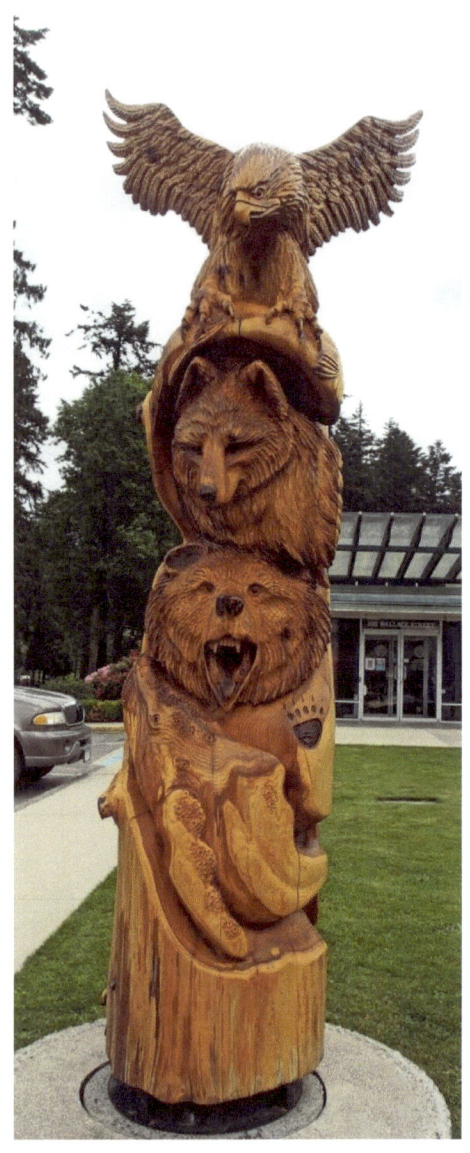

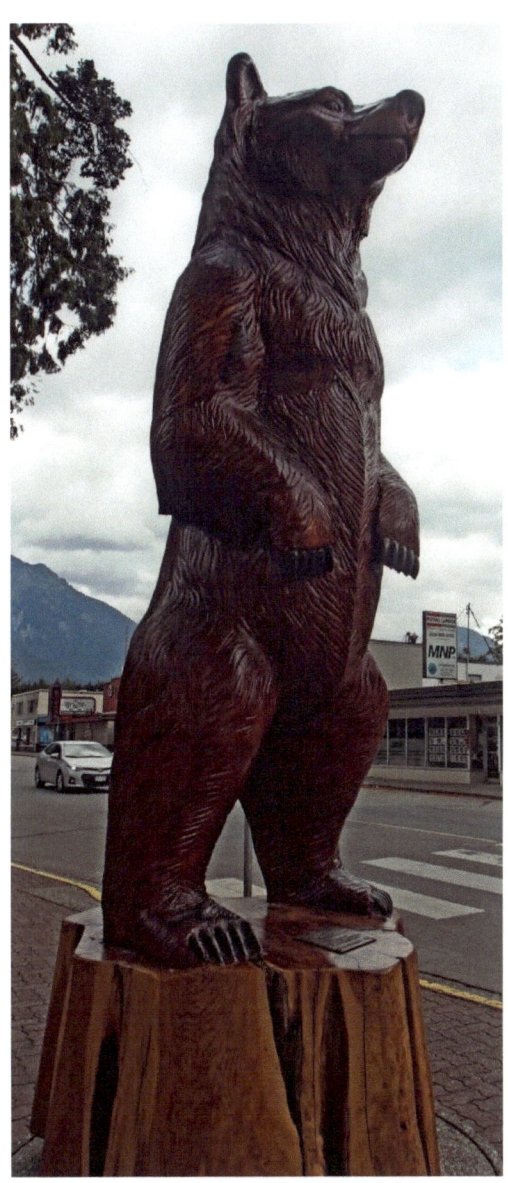

Carver: Pete Ryan 1992

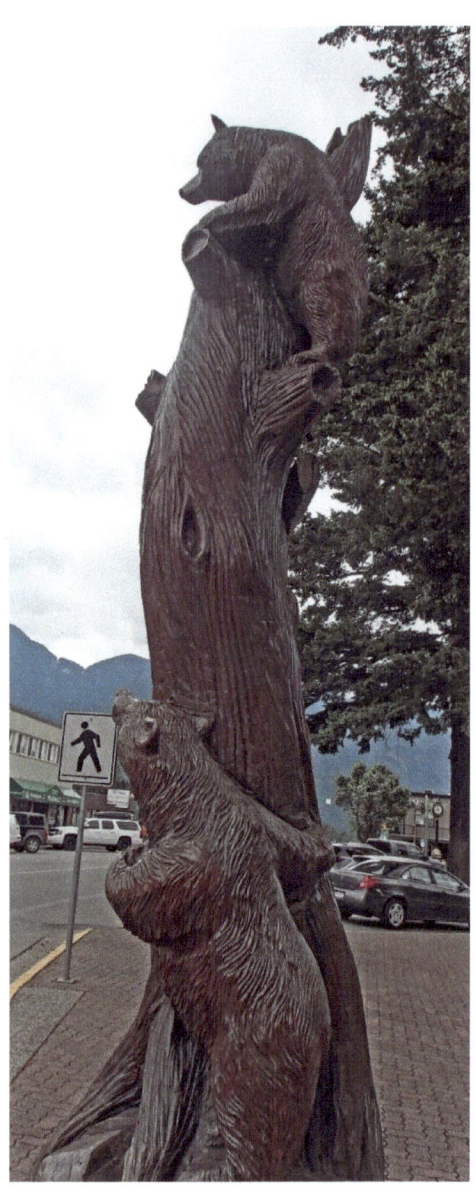

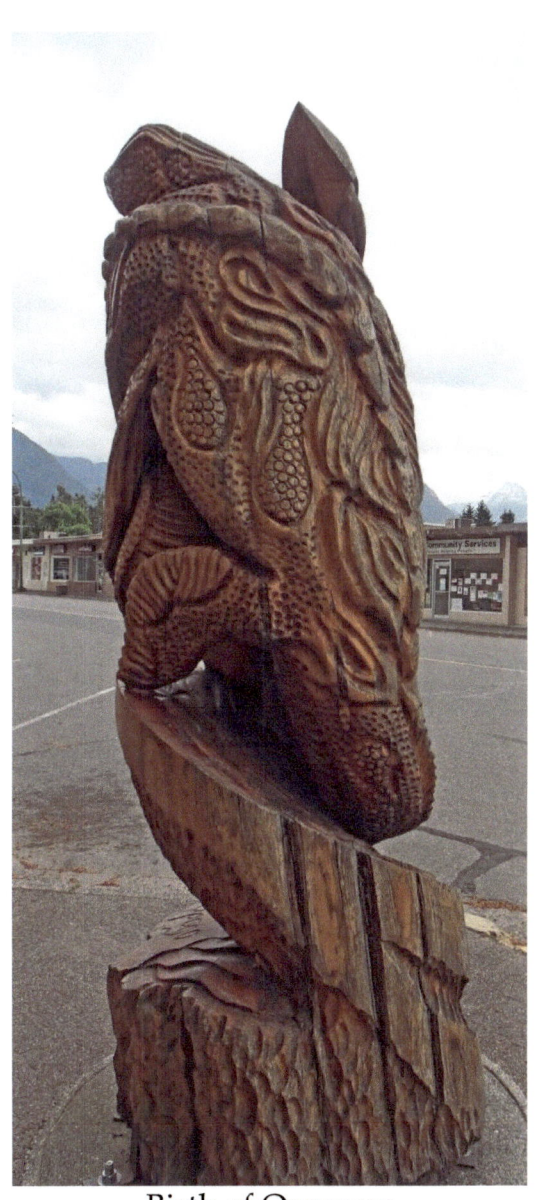

Birth of Ogopogo

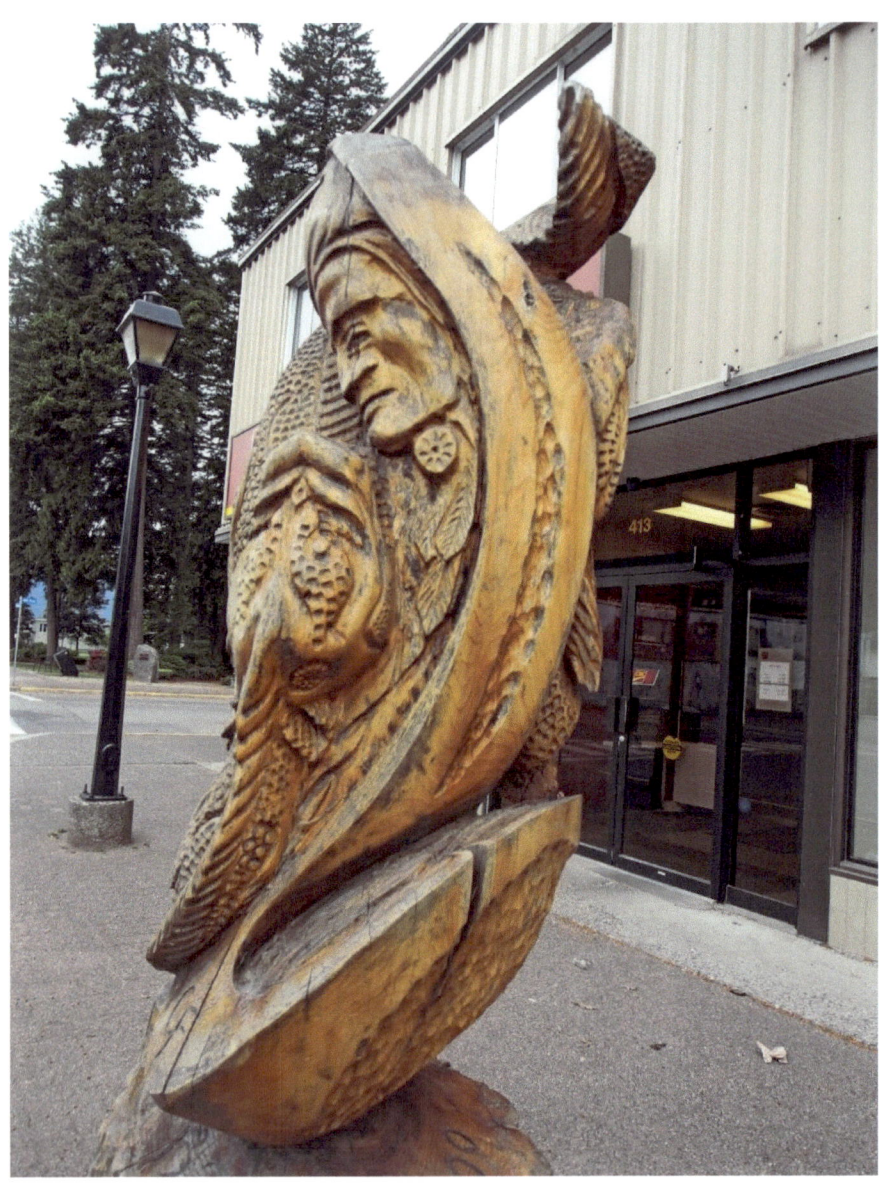

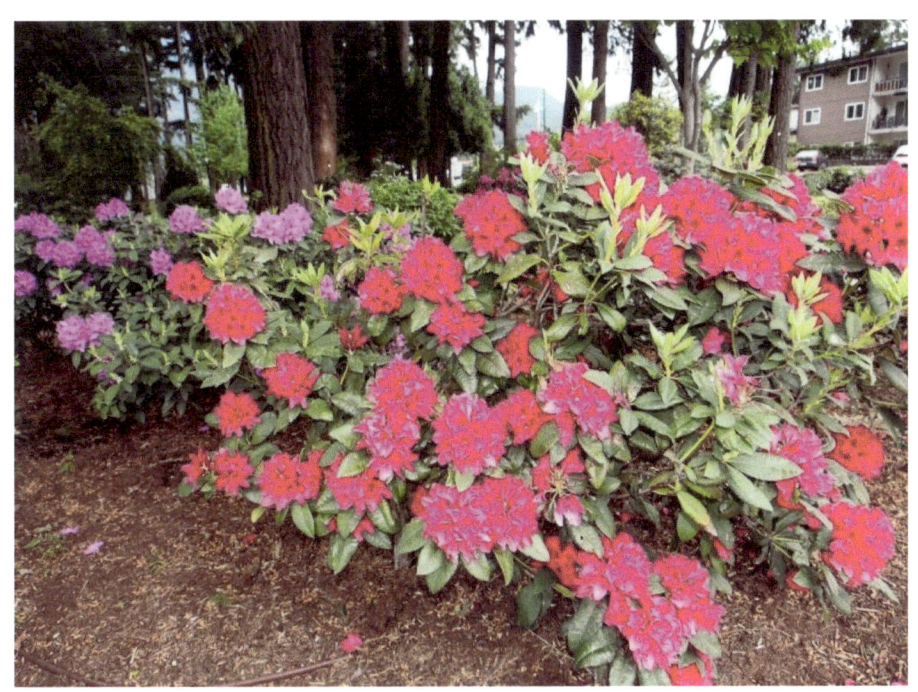

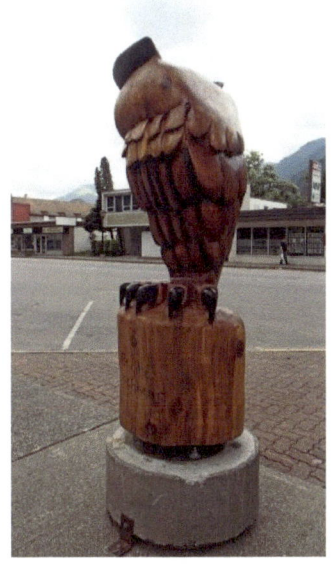

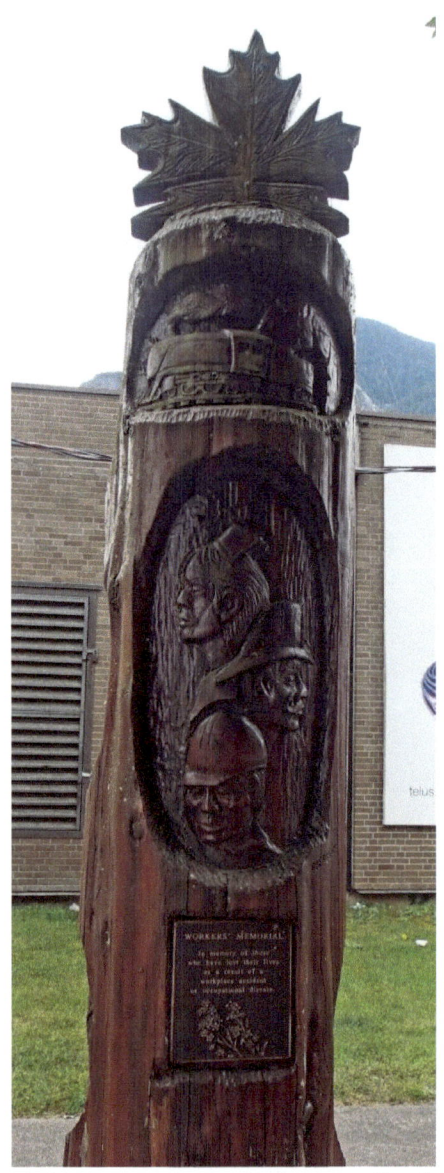

Workers' Memorial in memory of those who have lost their lives as a result of a workplace accident or occupational disease

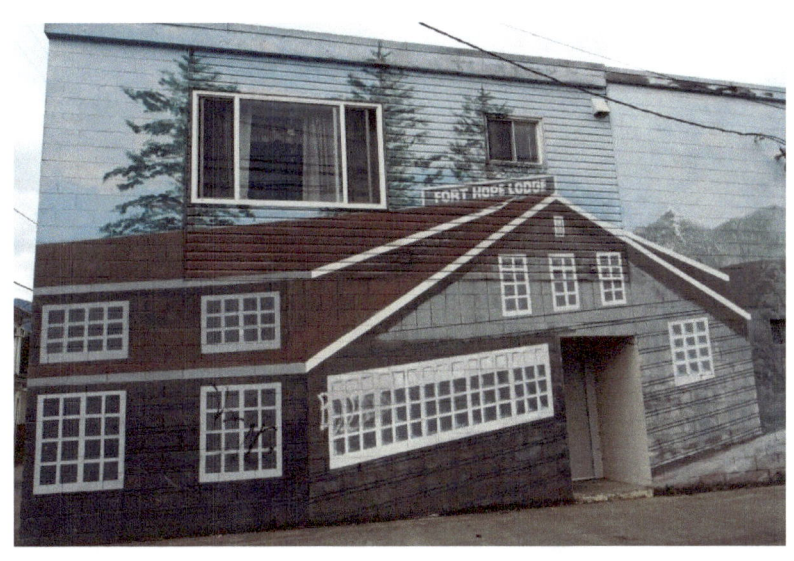

Mural by Razmpoosh Skoda 1996

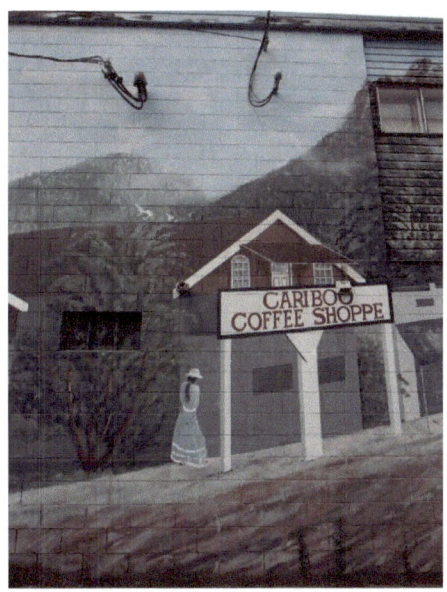

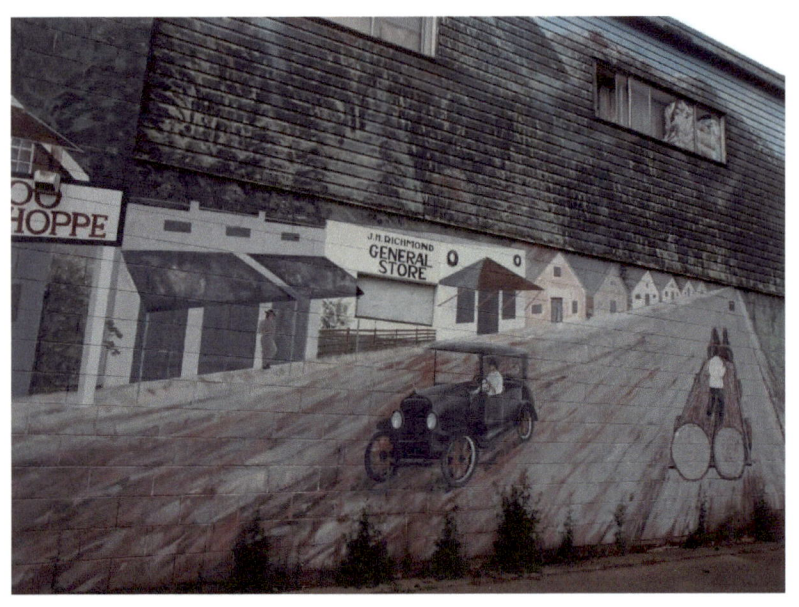

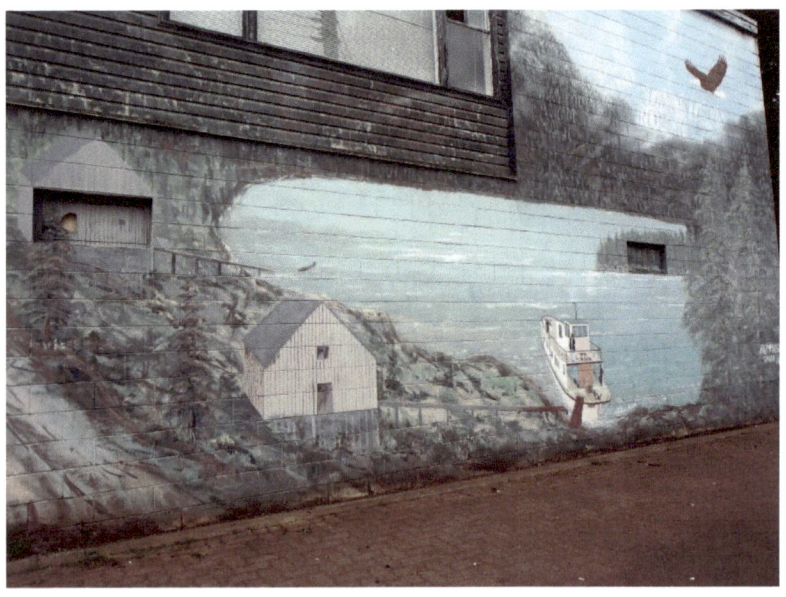

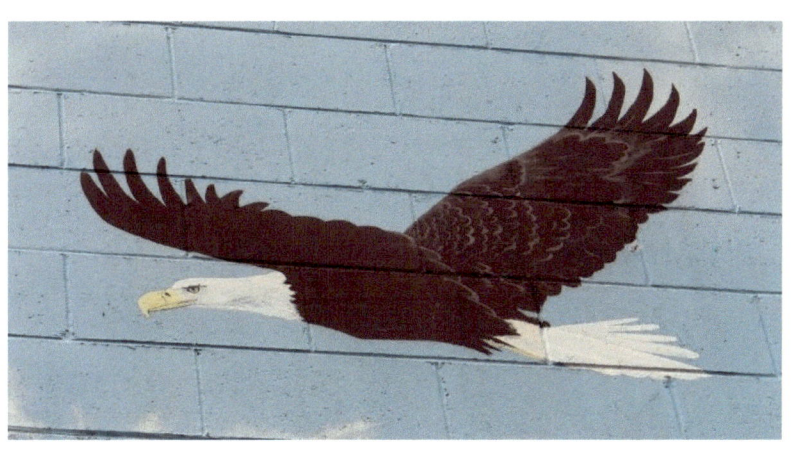

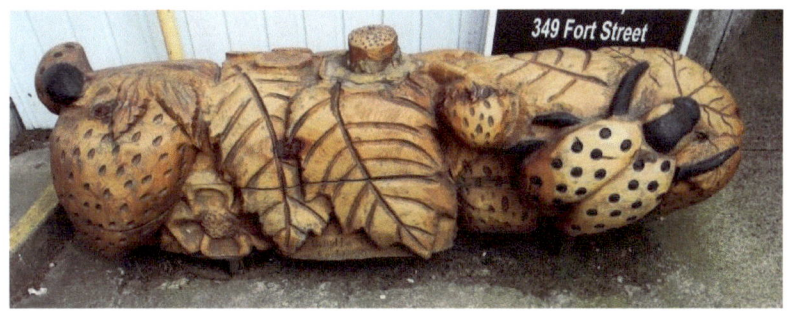

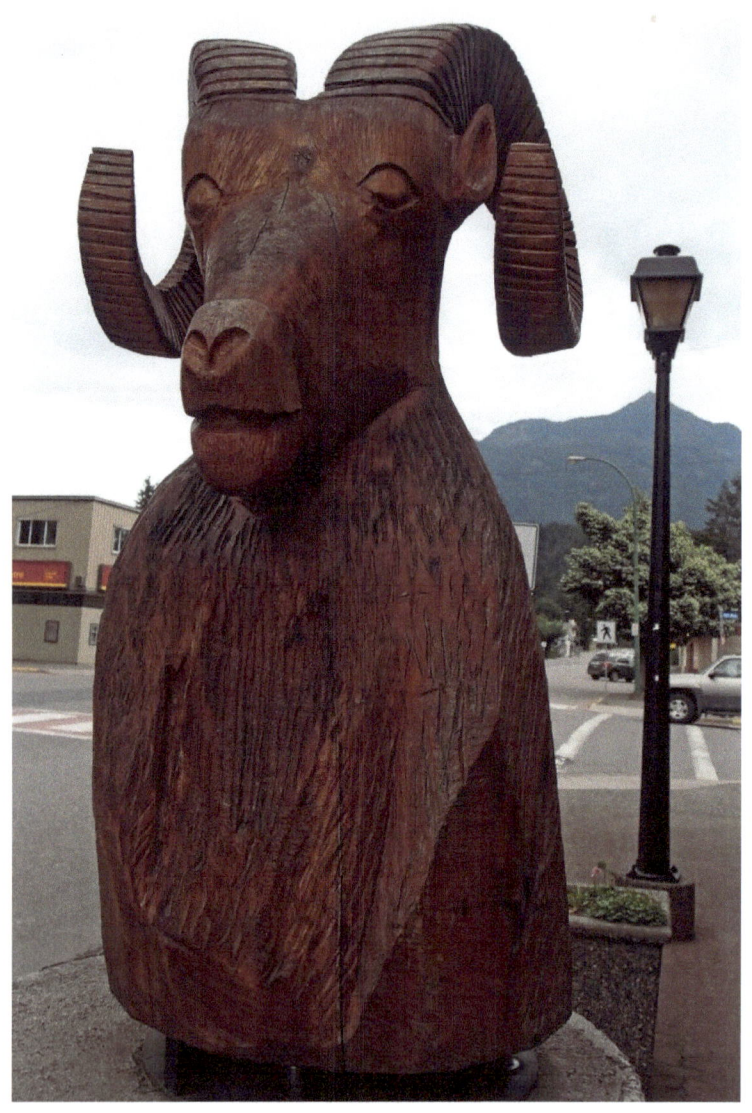

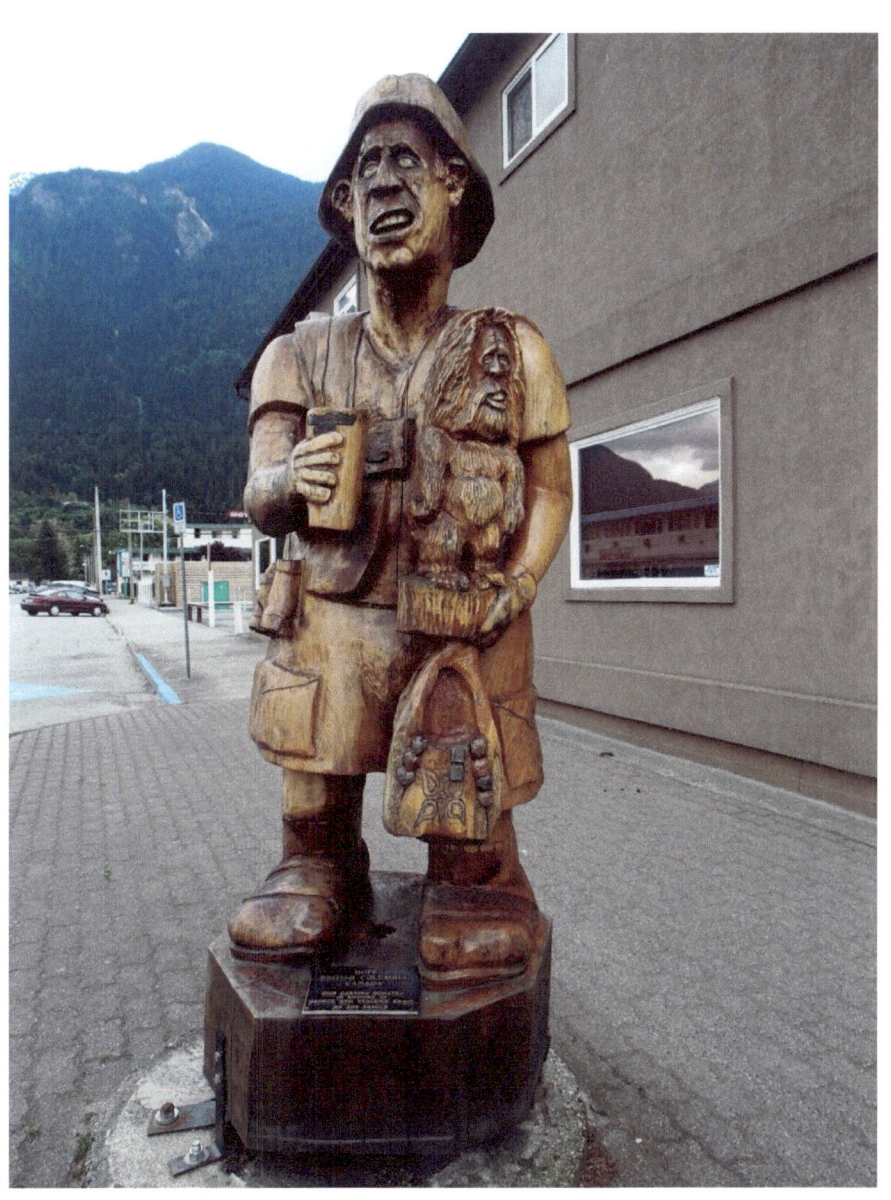

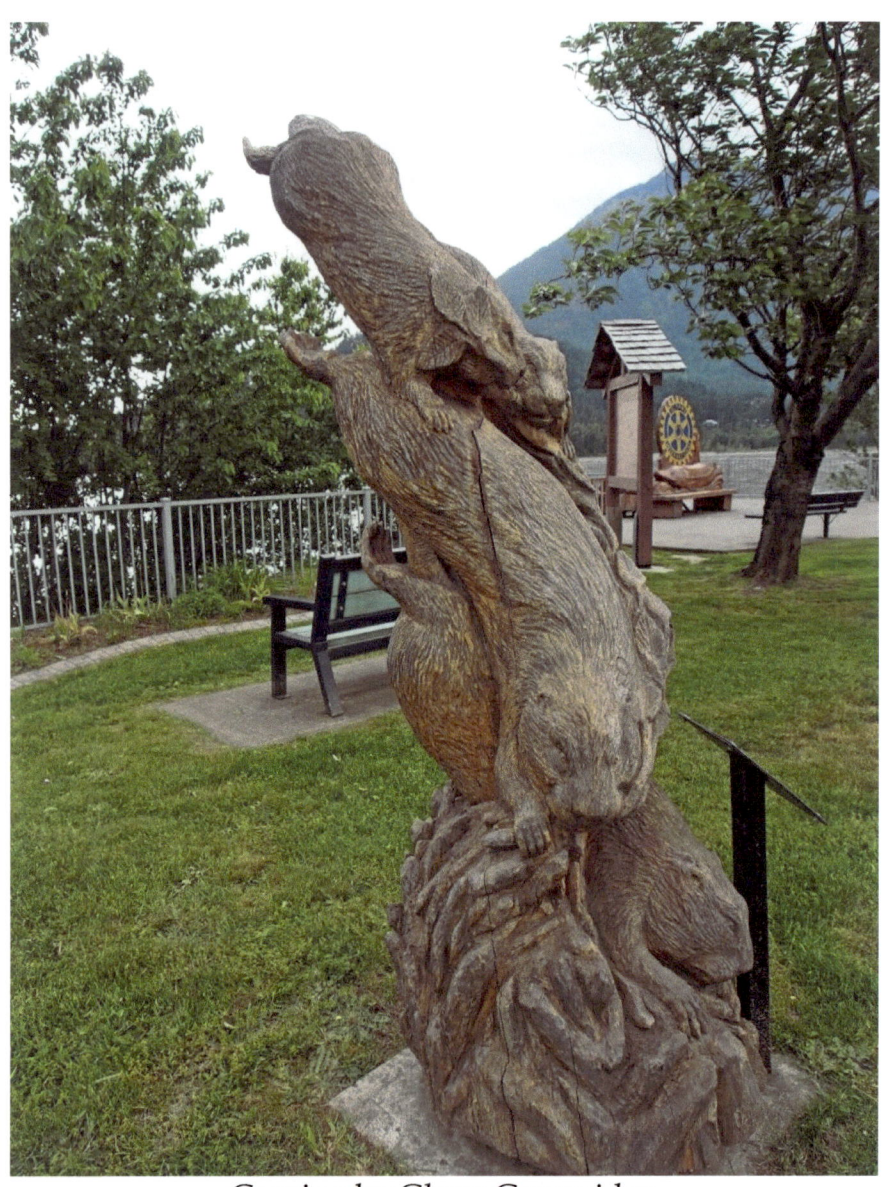
Carving by Glenn Greensides

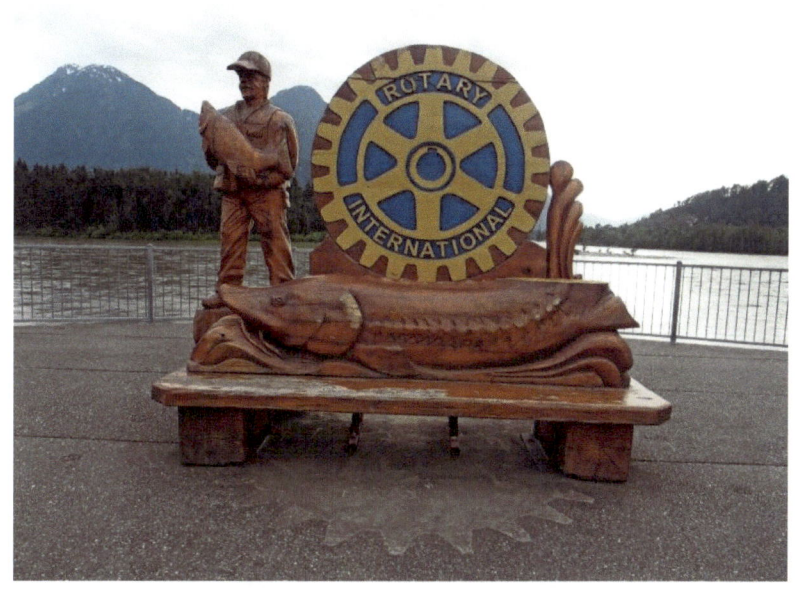
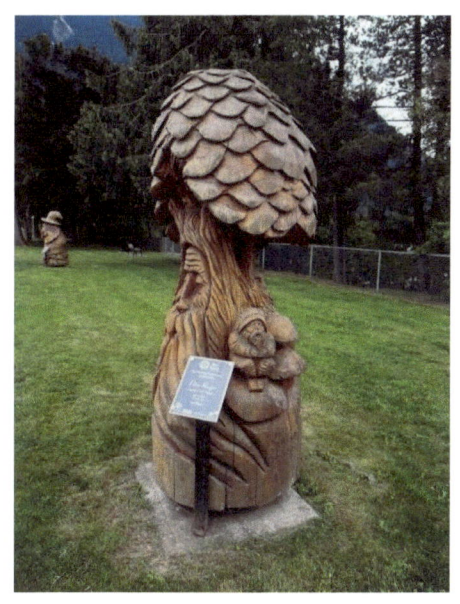

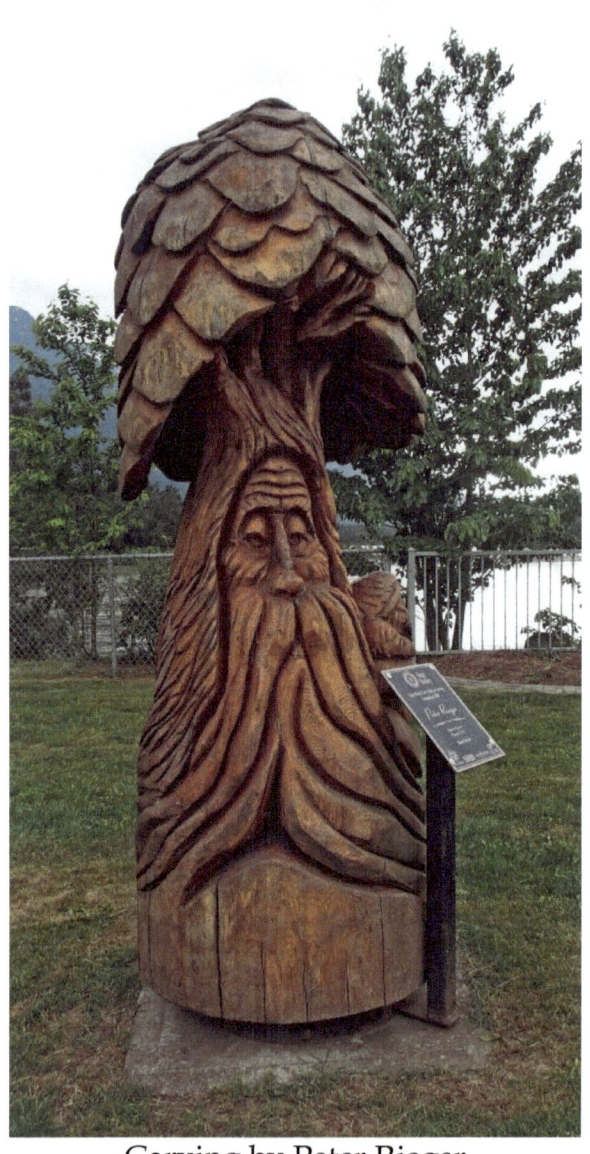

Carving by Peter Rieger

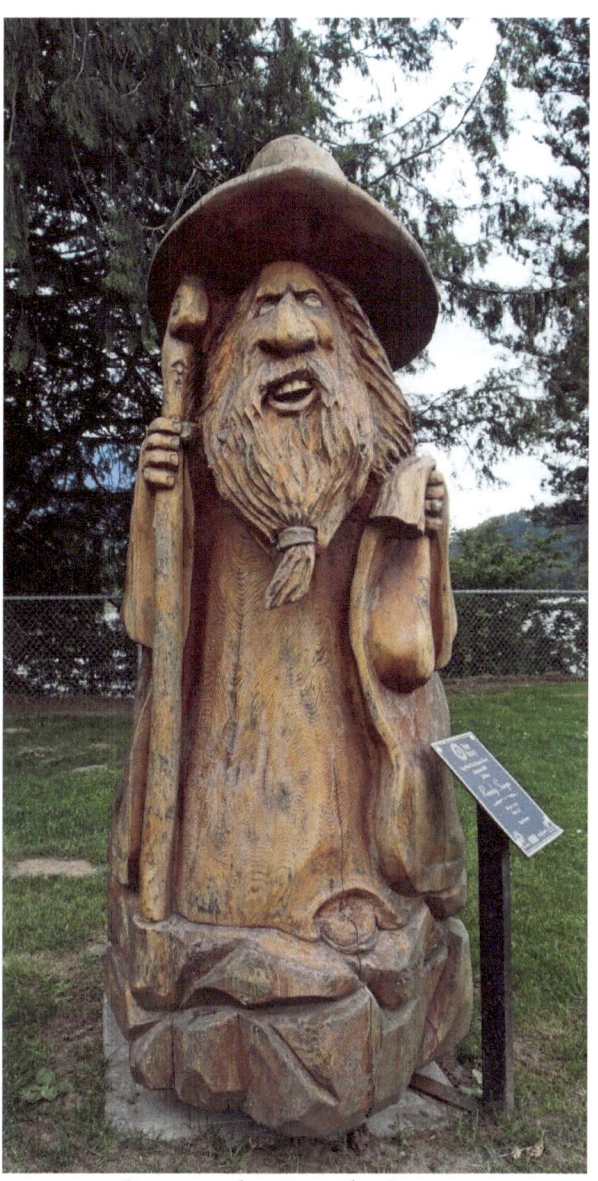

Carving by Randy Swope

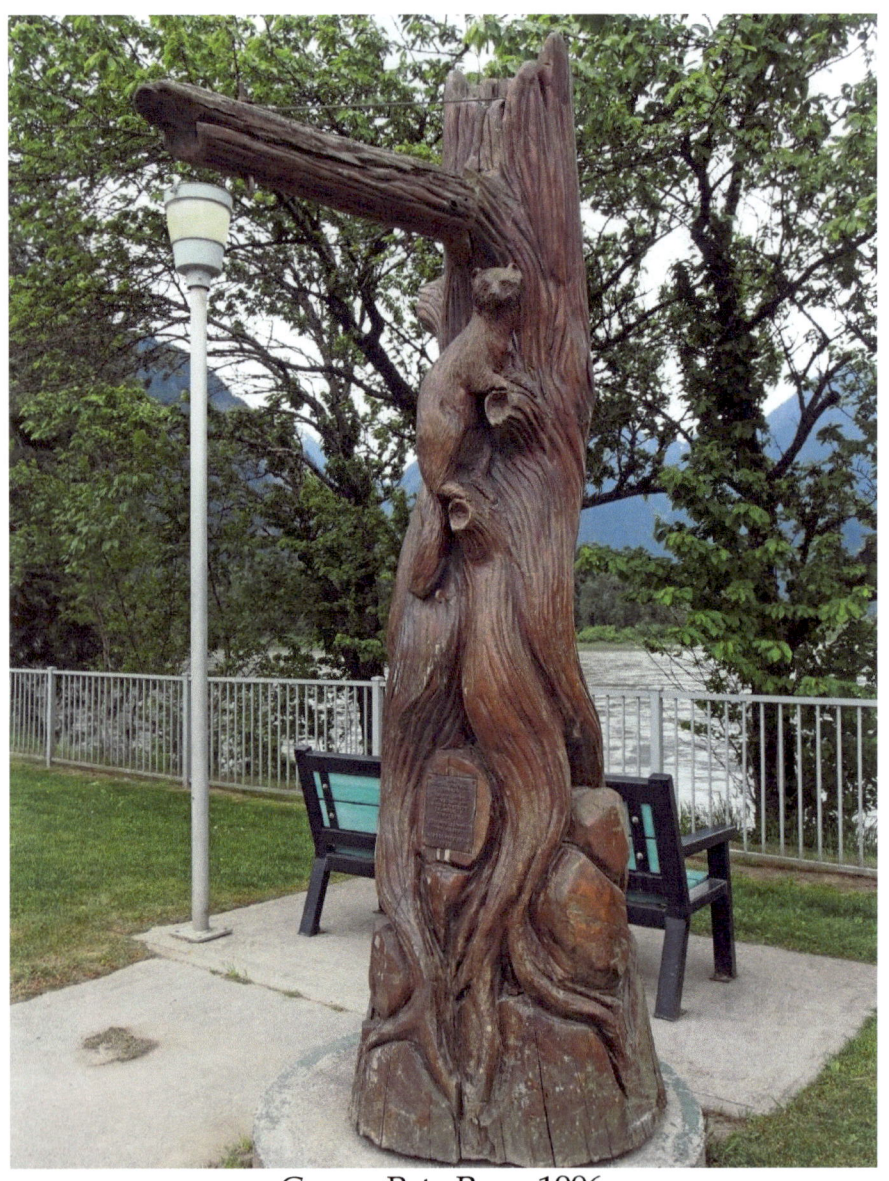

Carver Pete Ryan 1996

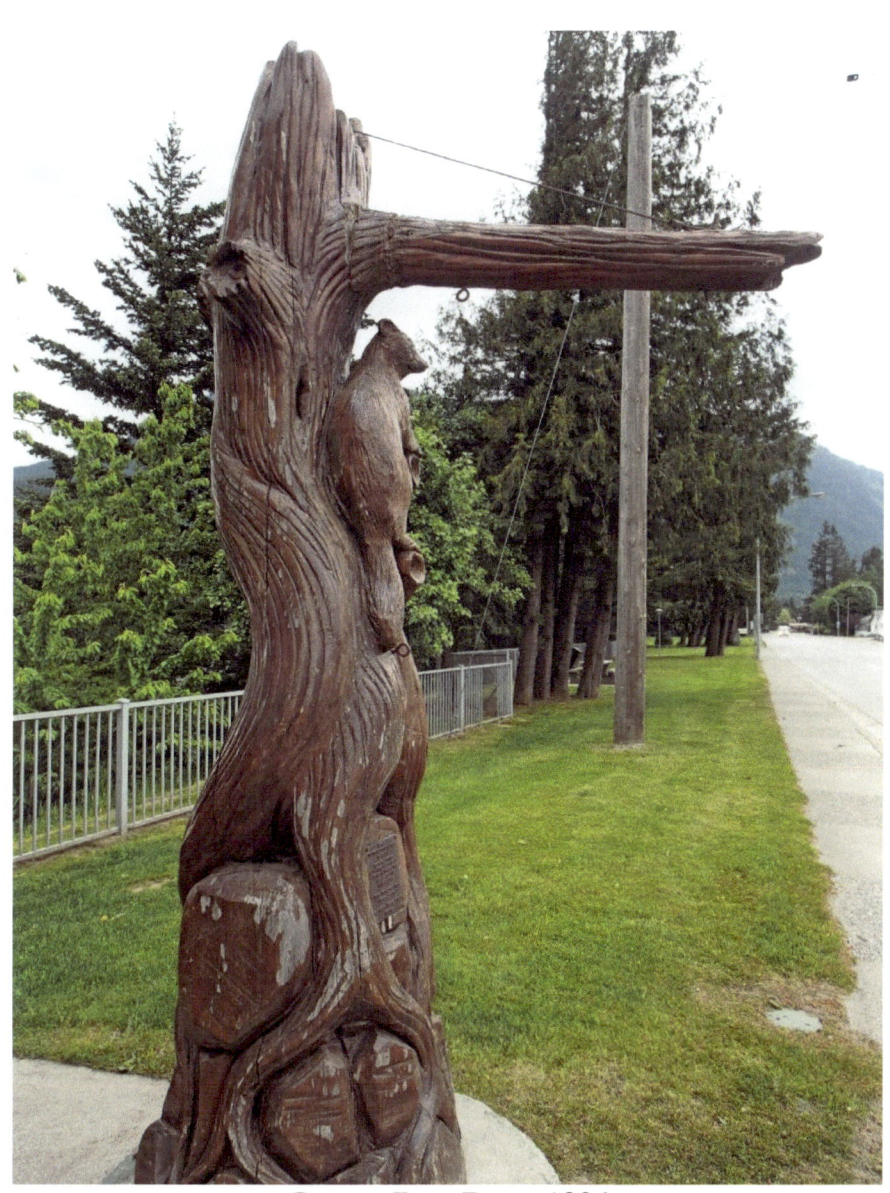

Carver Pete Ryan 1996

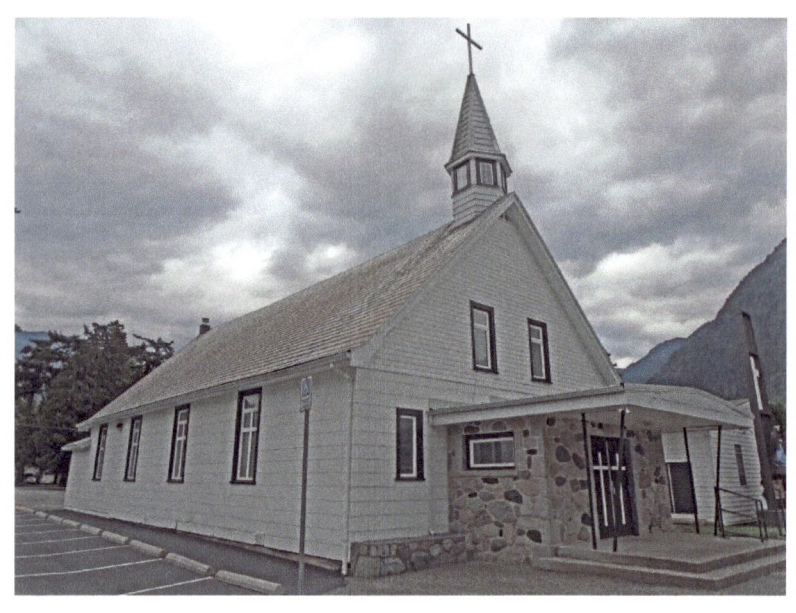

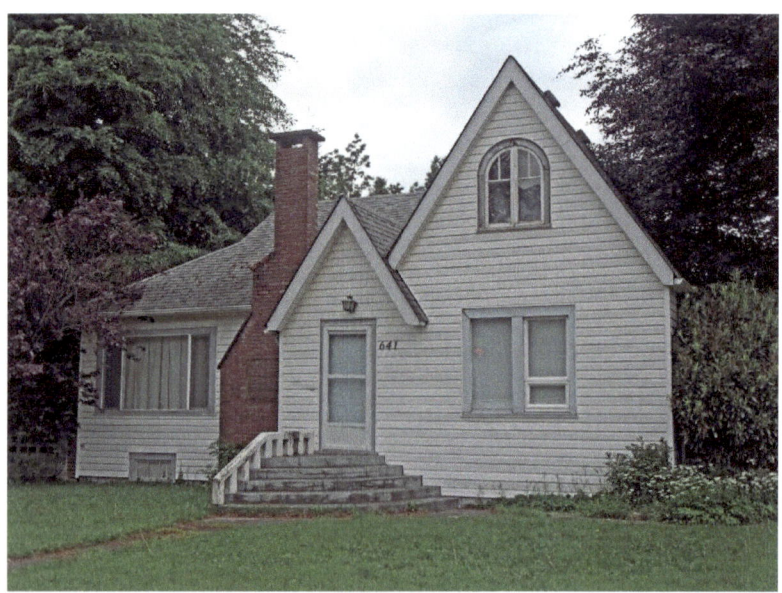

#641

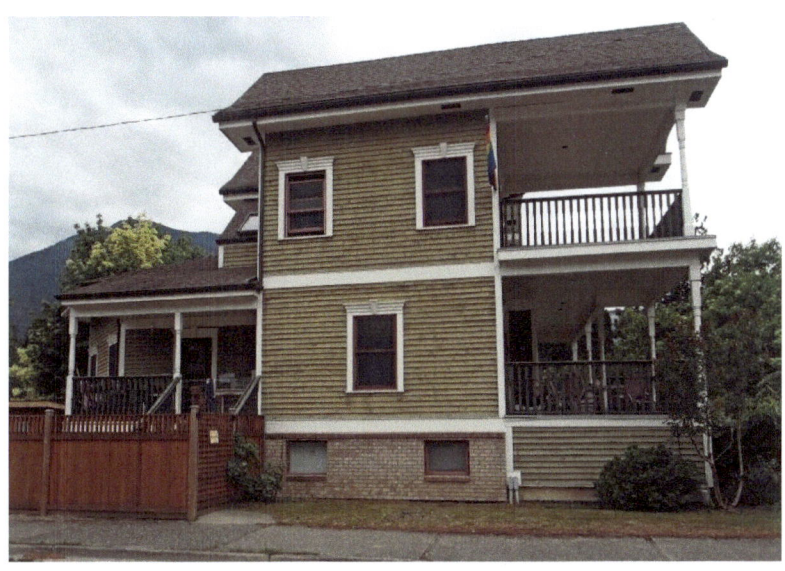

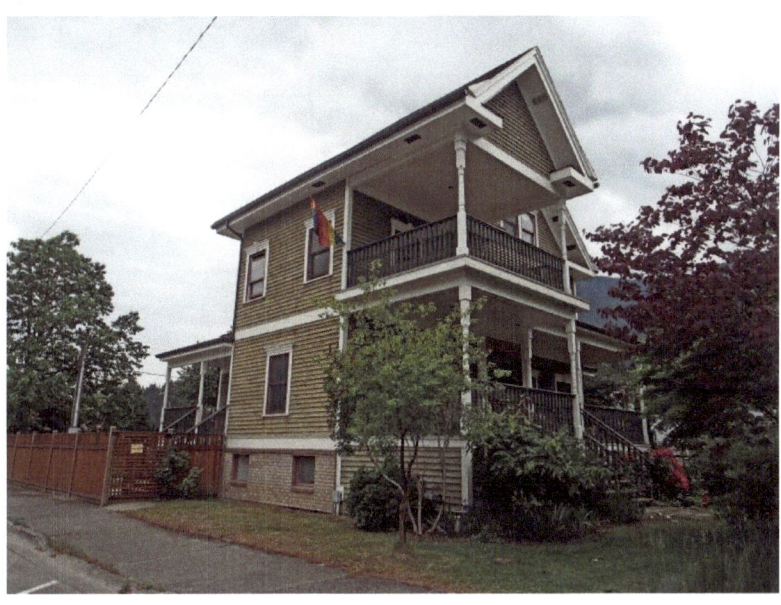

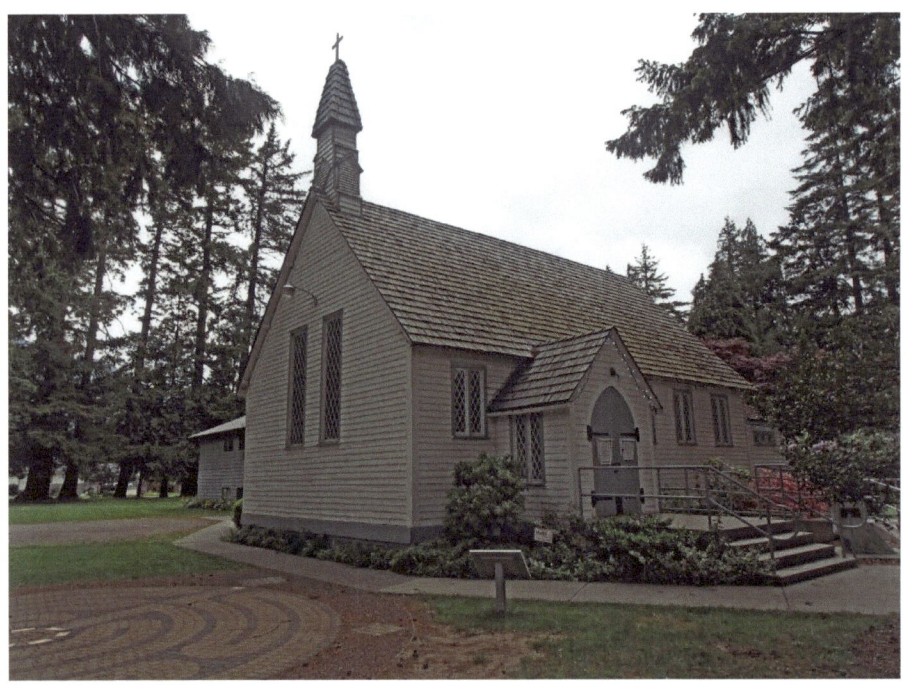

681 Fraser Avenue - Christ Church – 1861 – This white clapboard, Gothic Revival-styled Anglican Church with leaded glass windows first ministered to gold rush prospectors.

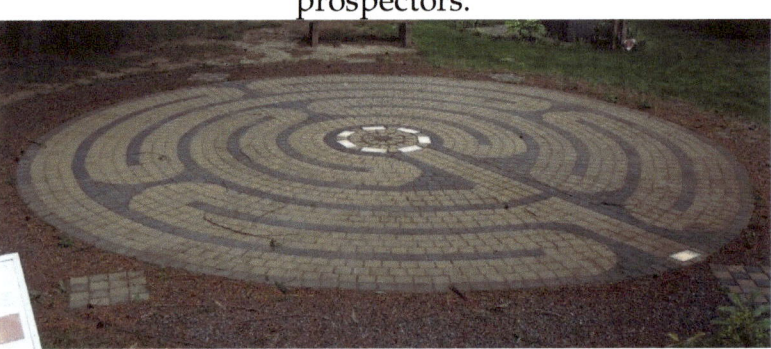

A Labyrinth consists of a single meandering pathway that leads from the entrance to the center and back out again. In the Christian tradition, it is a place where one can experience a spiritual walk with our creator. It provides a time for private meditation, a time to pray and talk to God.

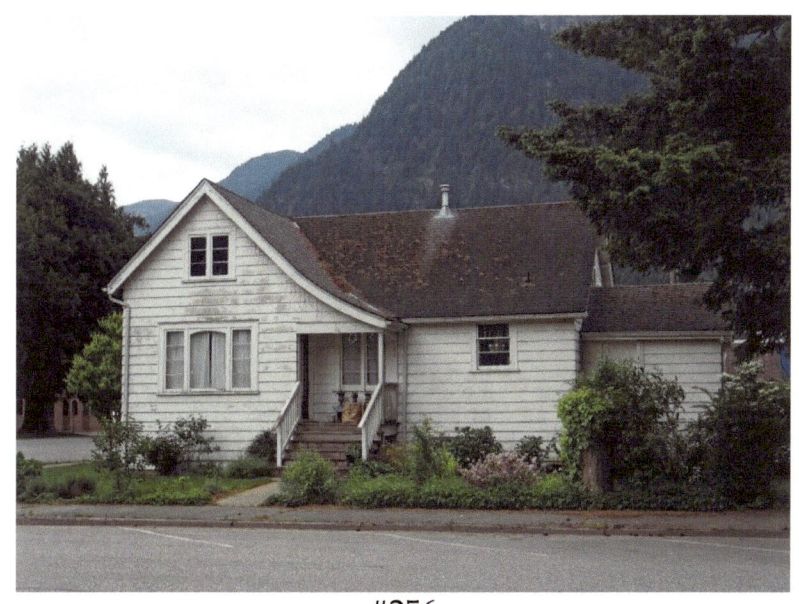

#256

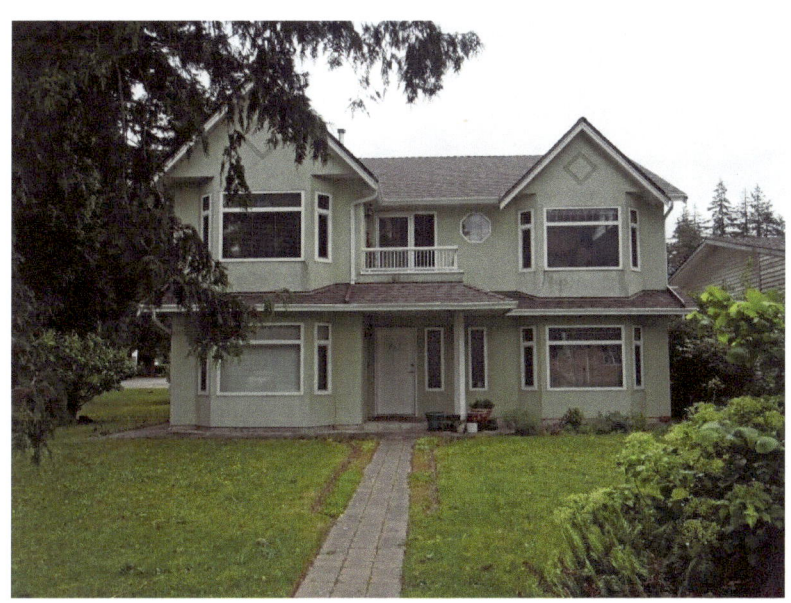

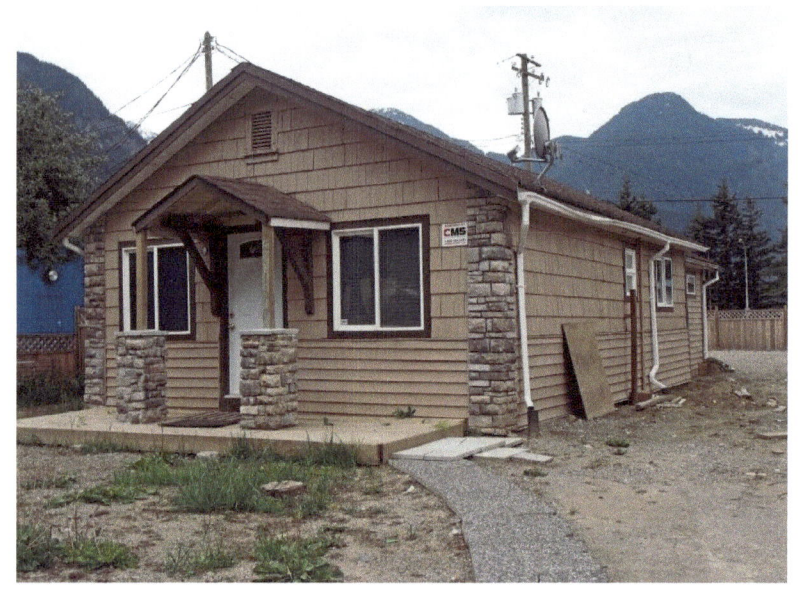

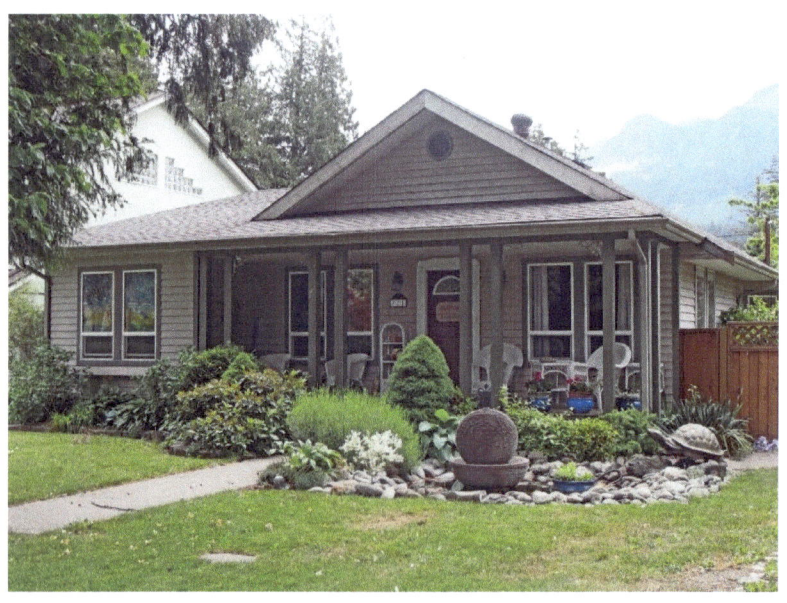

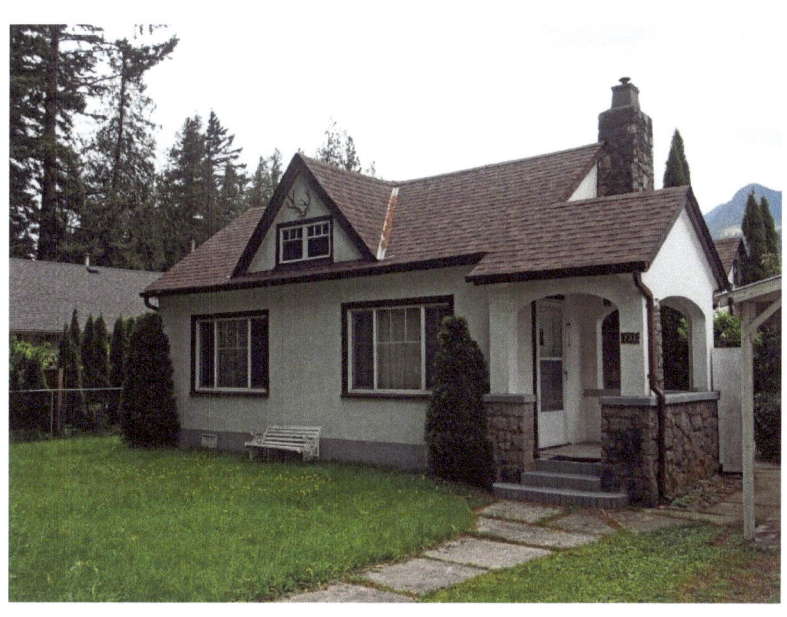

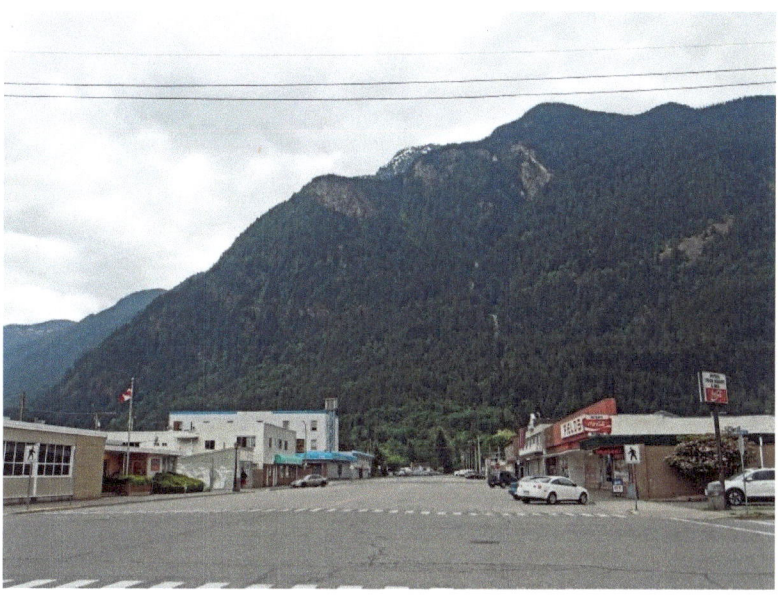

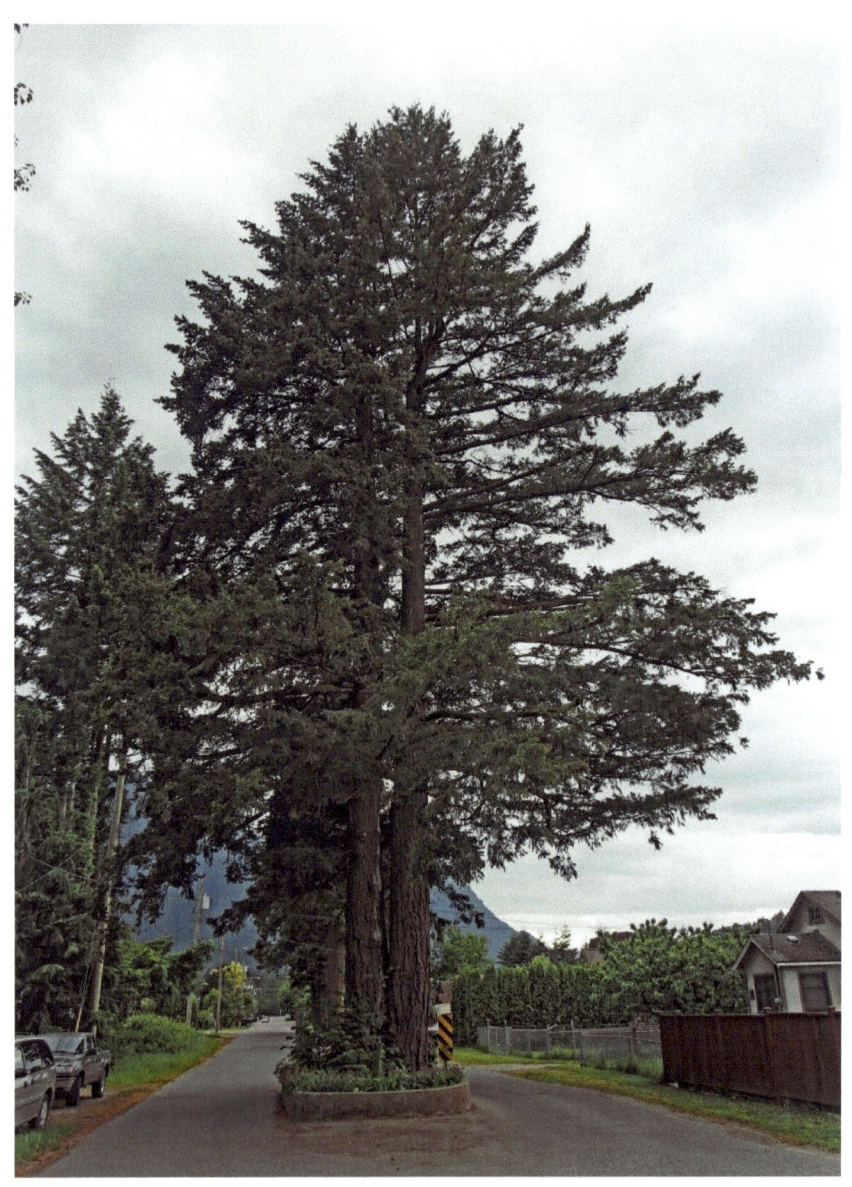

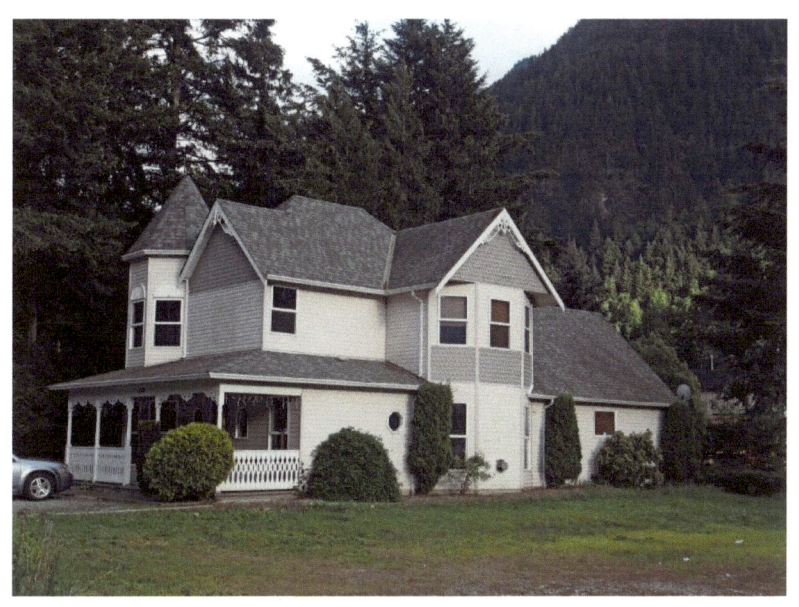
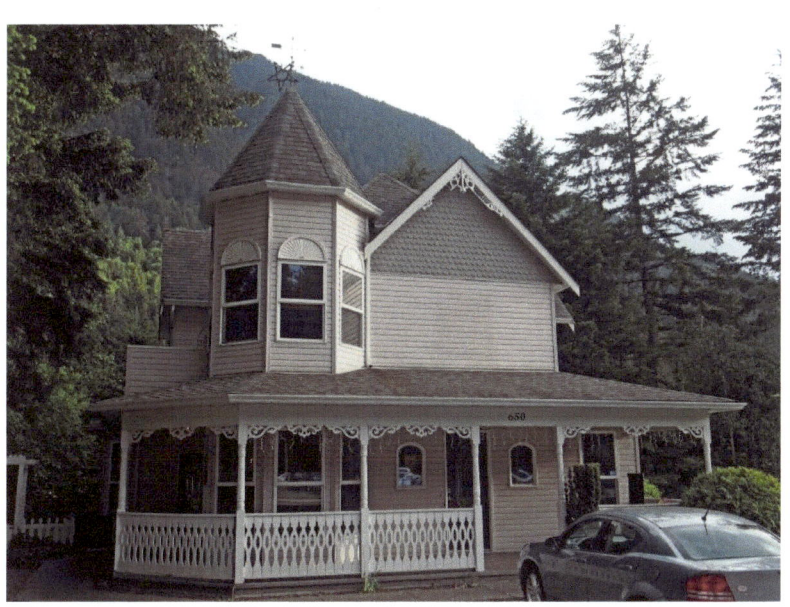

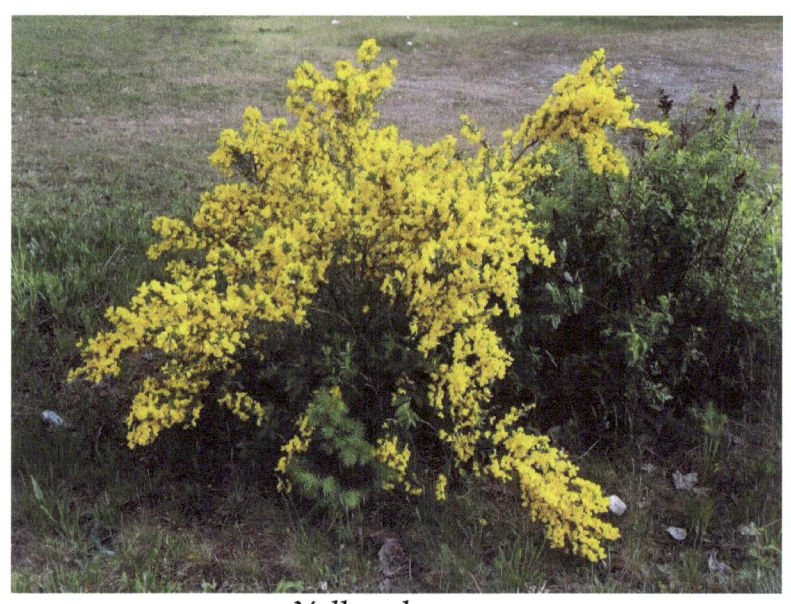

Yellow broom

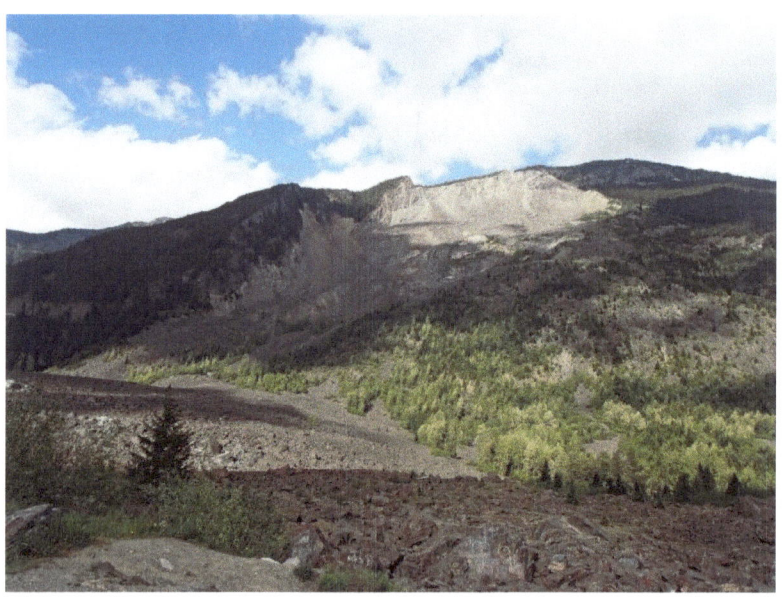

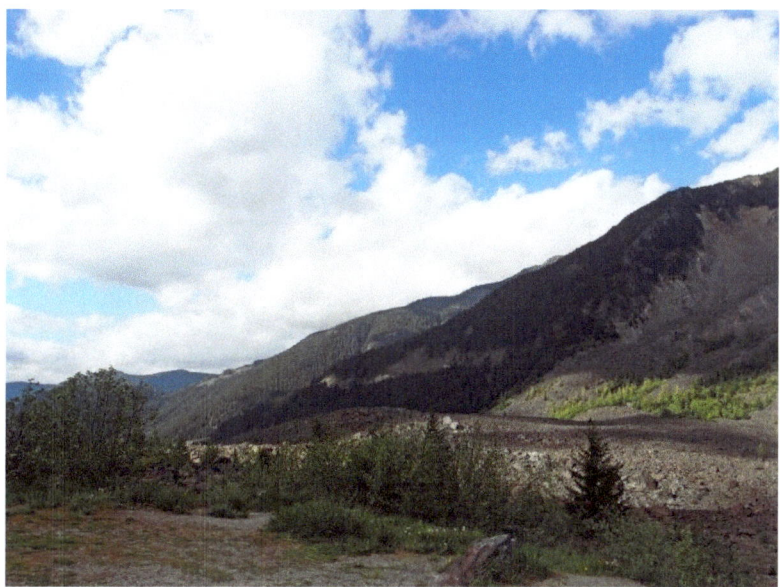

Early January 9, 1965 a huge landslide occurred and destroyed about three kilometers of the Hope-Princeton Highway. The slide, consisting of more than 46 million cubic meters of earth, rock and snow, crashed down in seconds from the 2,000 meter high mountain ridge.

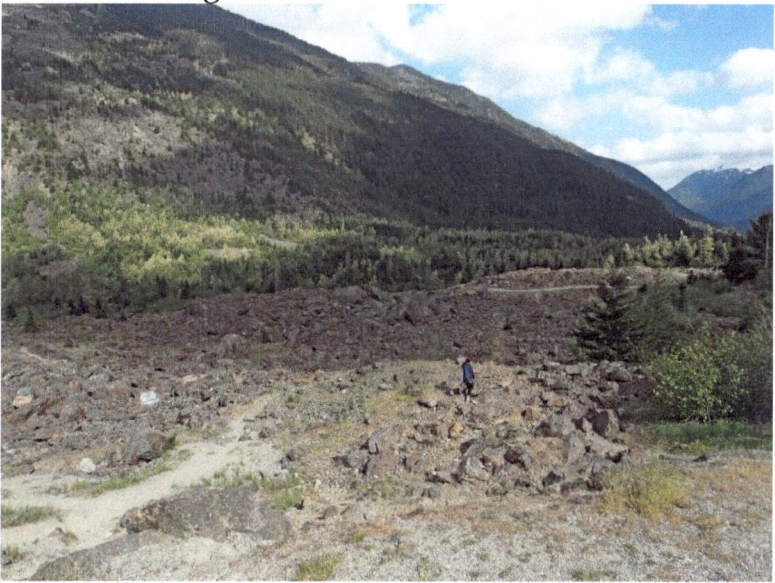

Princeton

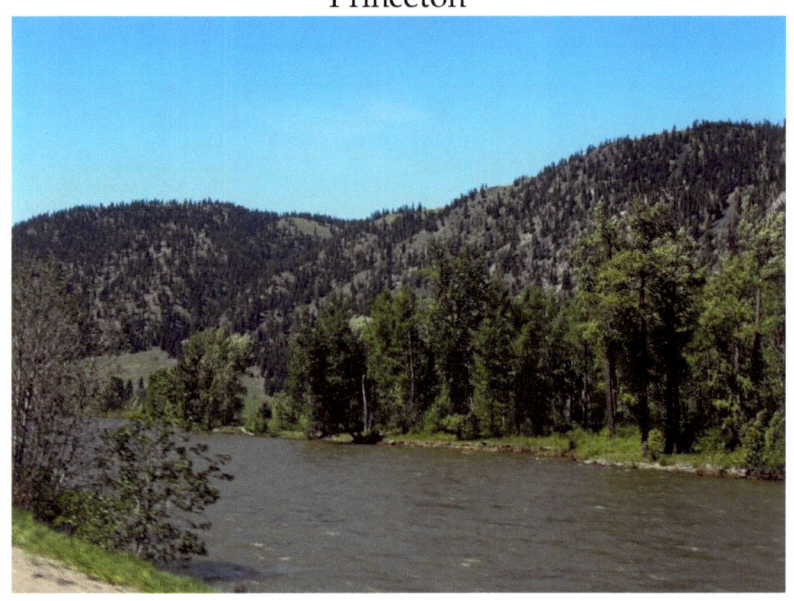

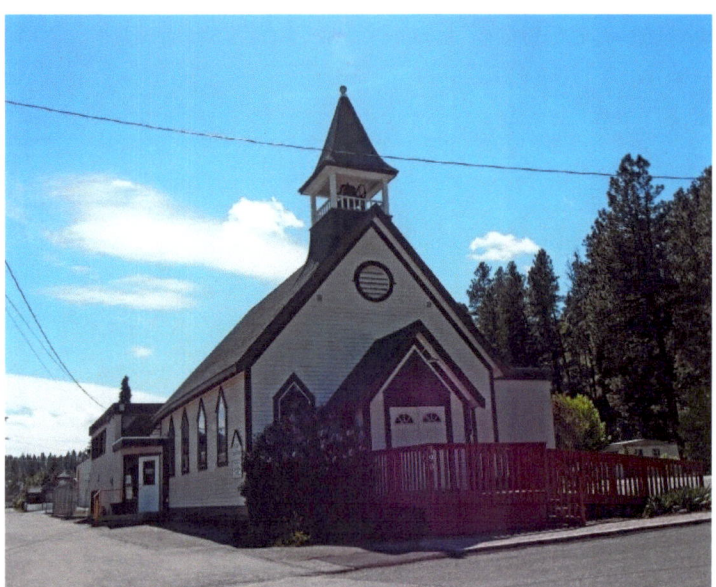

St. John's United Church, Princeton – Gothic

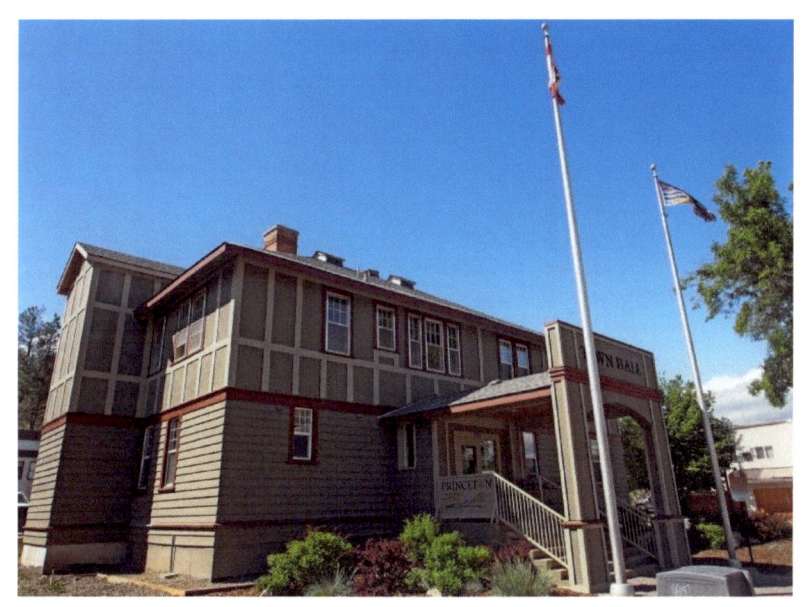

Princeton Town Hall

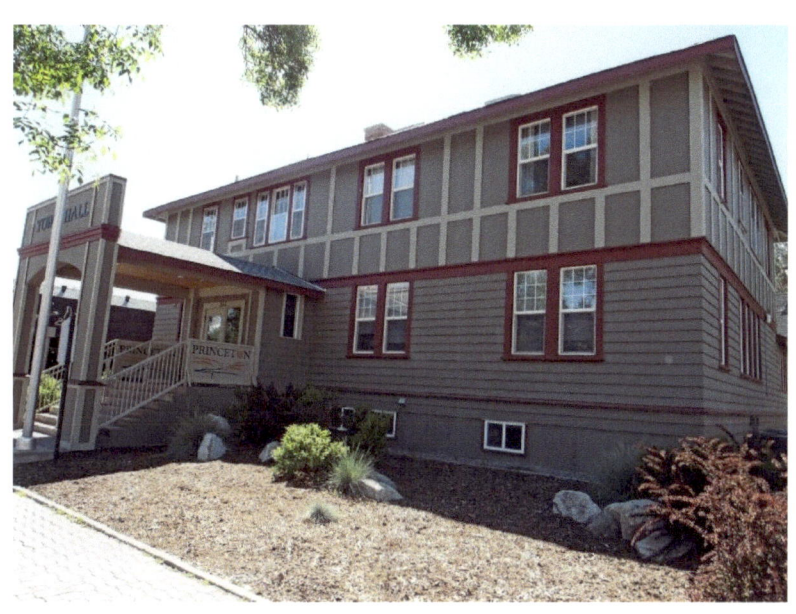

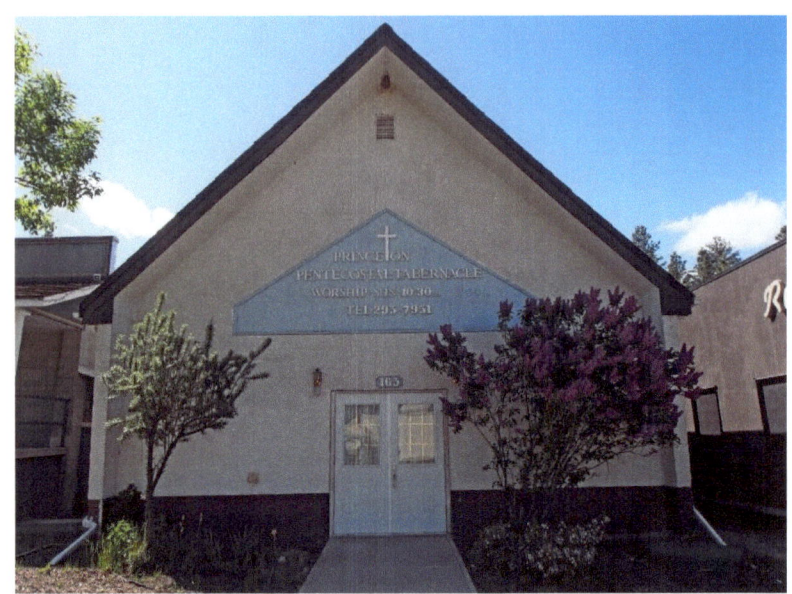

Princeton Pentecostal Tabernacle

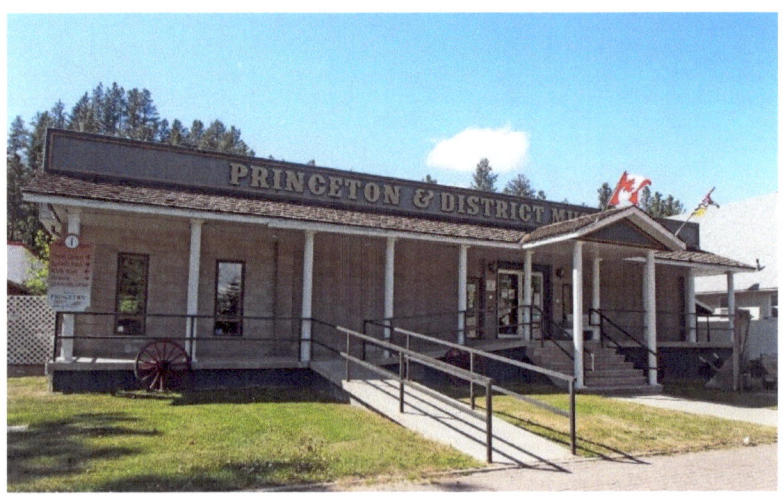

Princeton & District Museum

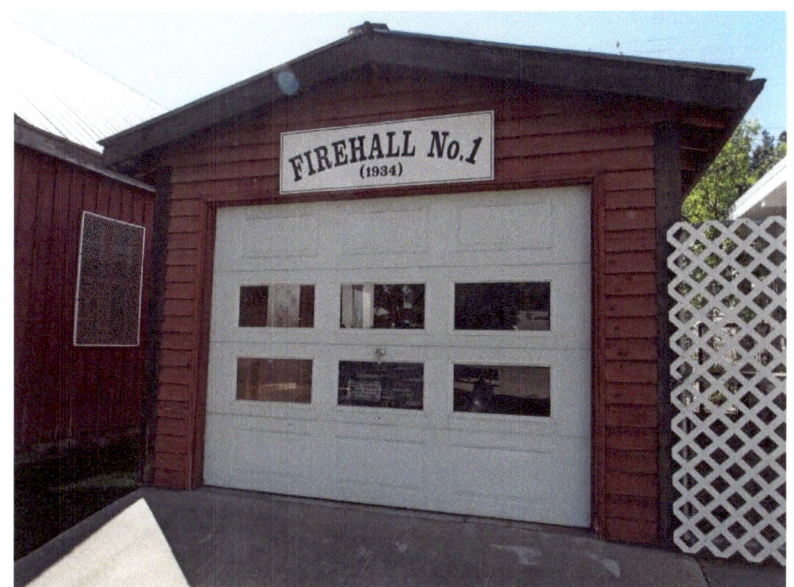

Fire Hall

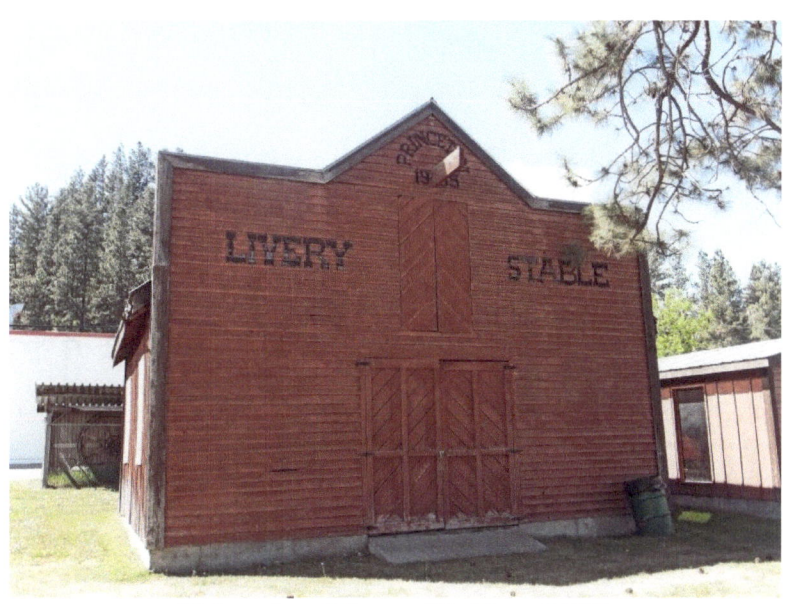

Princeton Livery Stable – 1935

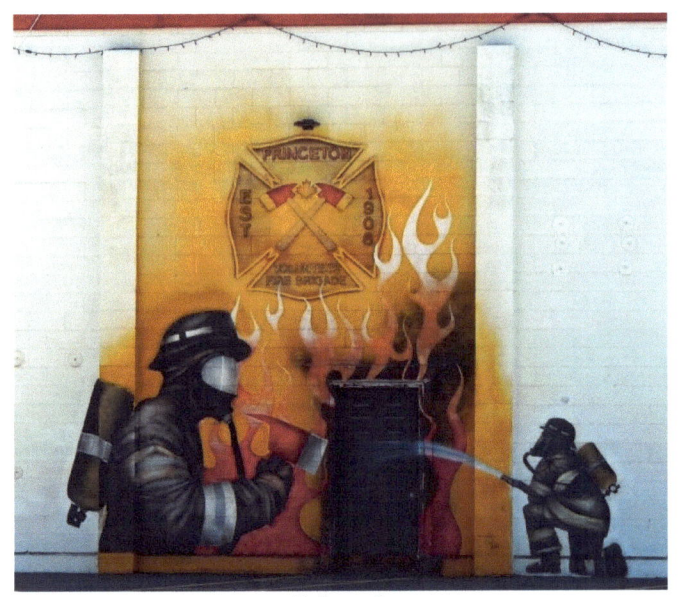
Mural

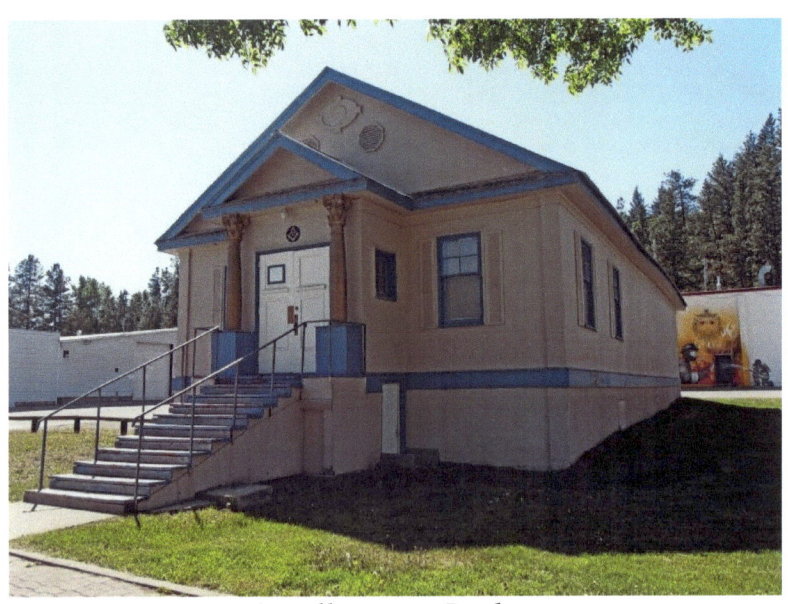
Similkameen Lodge

Hedley

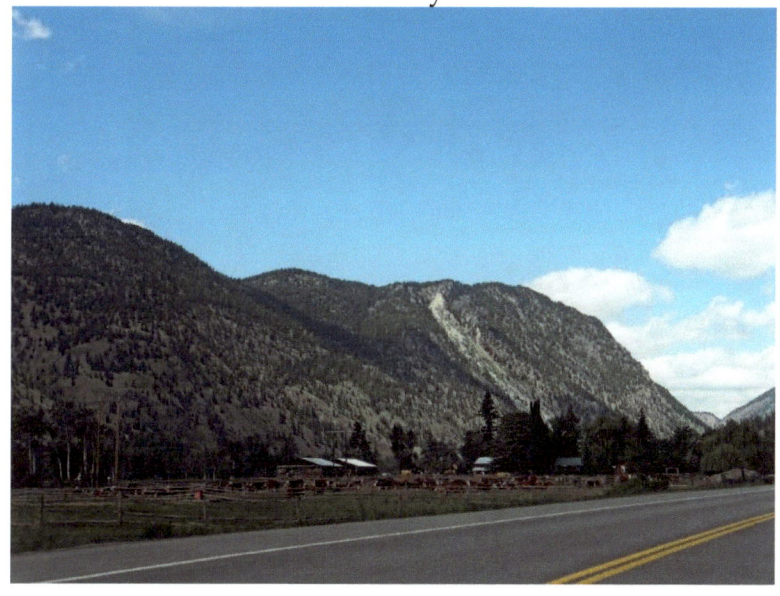

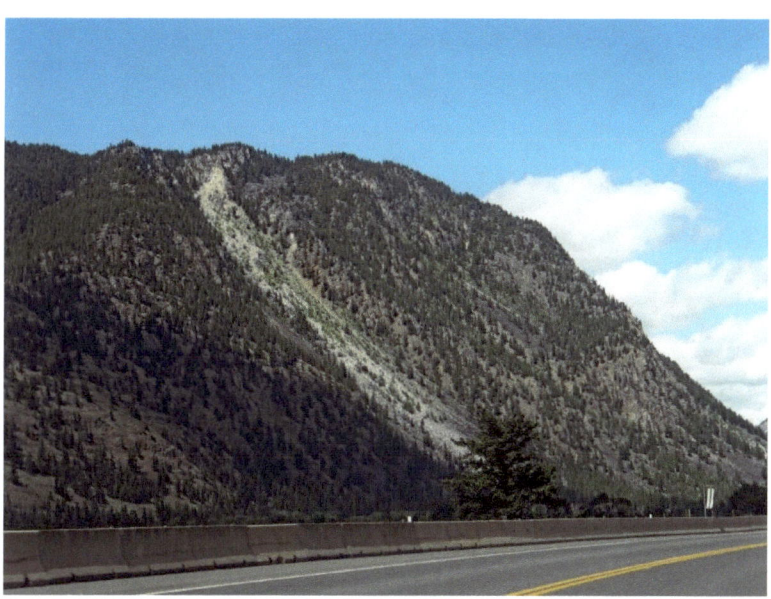

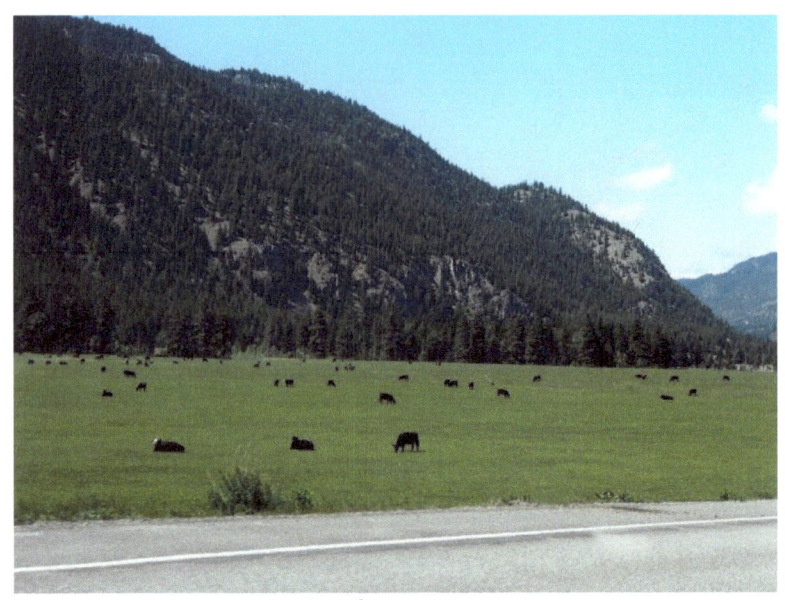
Cattle grazing

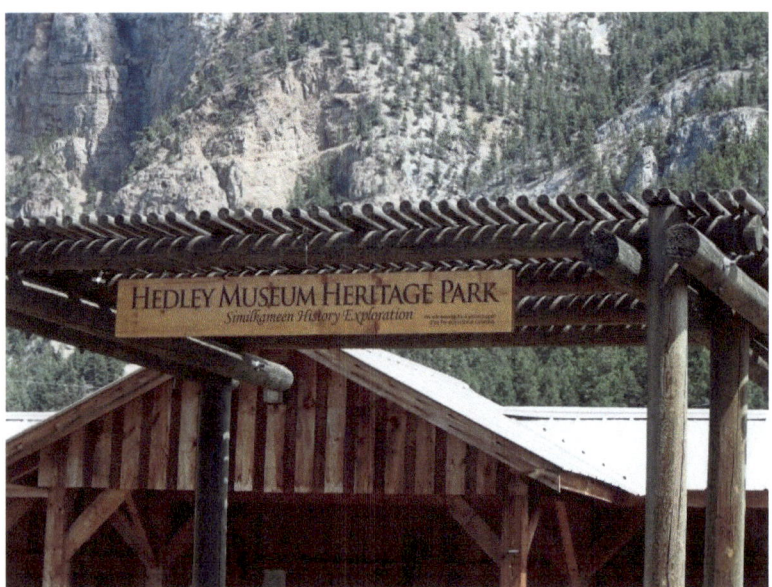
Hedley Museum Heritage Park

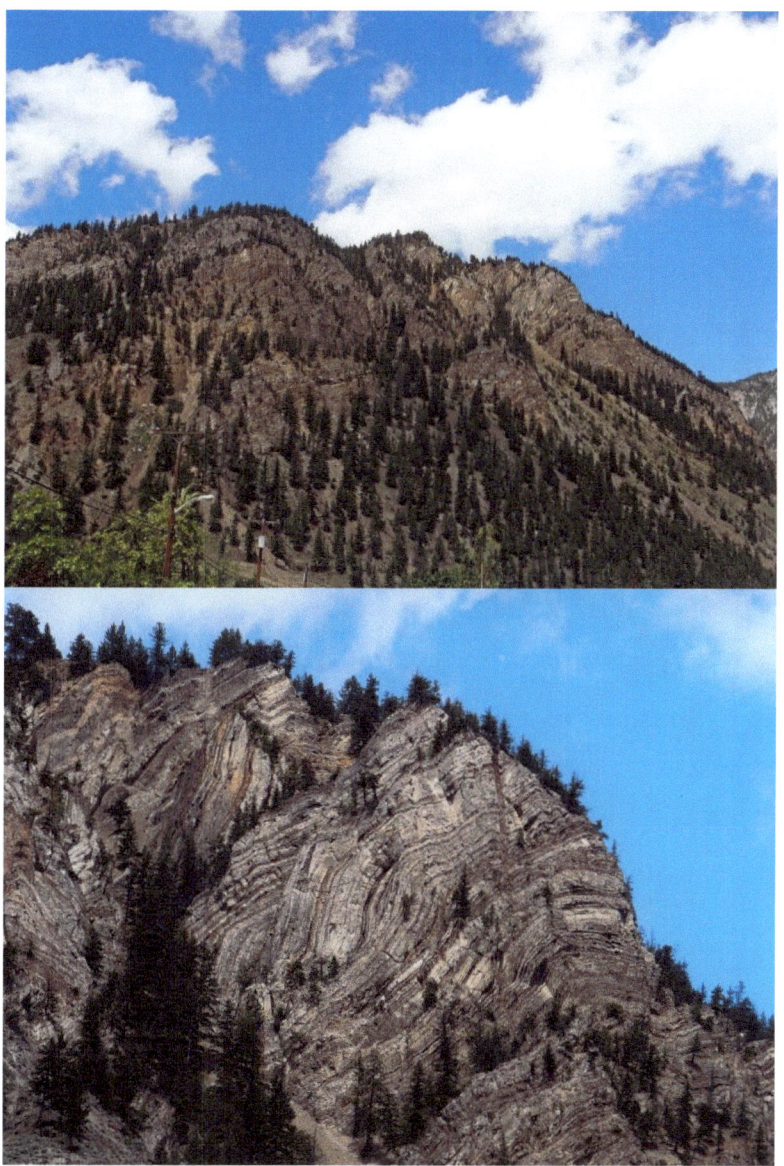

From the heart of this mountain, men took $47,000,000 in gold. In 1904 Hedley boomed with the opening of the mill in town and the Nickel Plate Mine on the mountaintop. The nearby Hedley Mascot Mine, on a claim of less than an acre, mined a fortune. In 1955 the gold, silver and copper ore was exhausted.

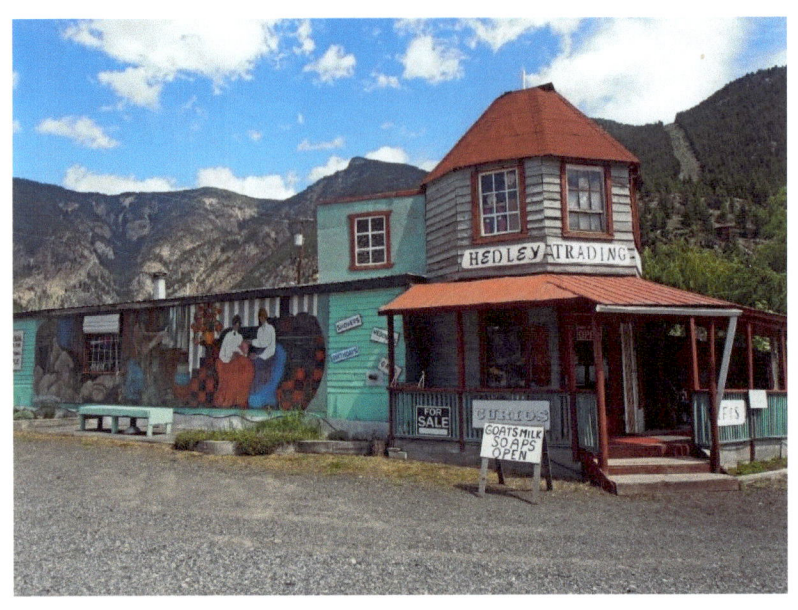

Hedley Trading Post

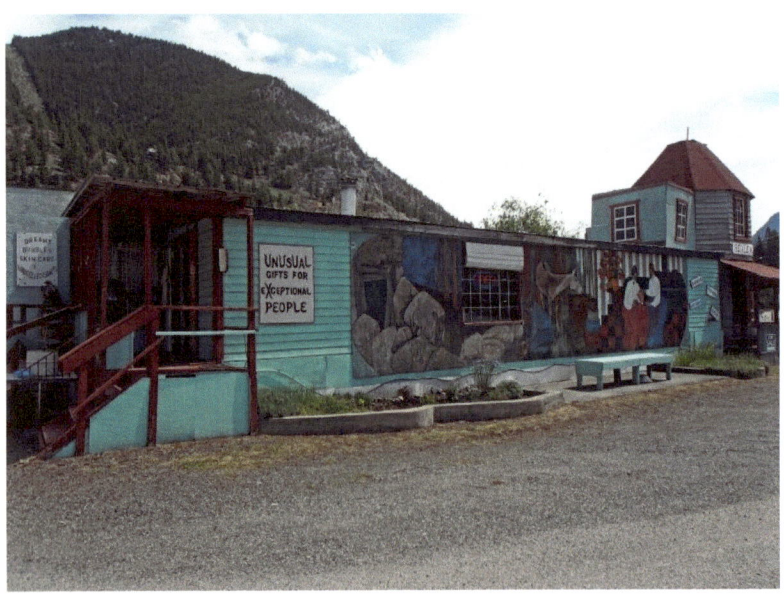

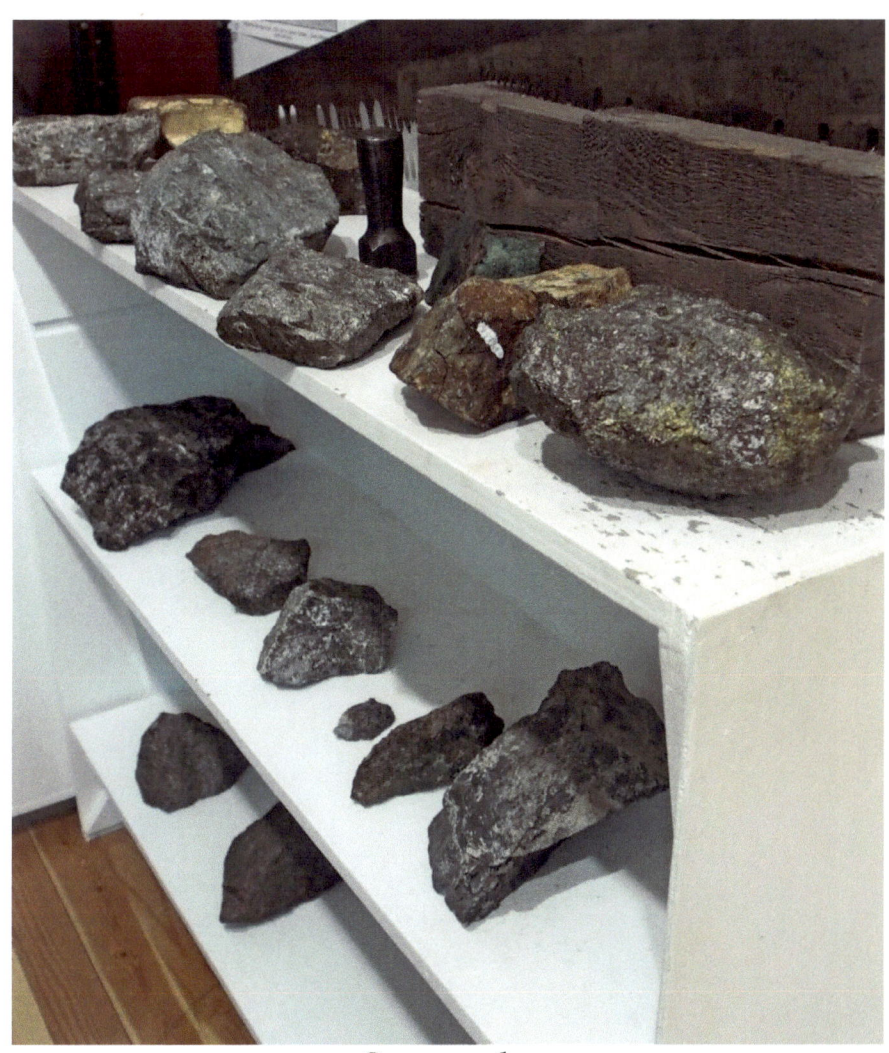

Ore samples

Keremeos

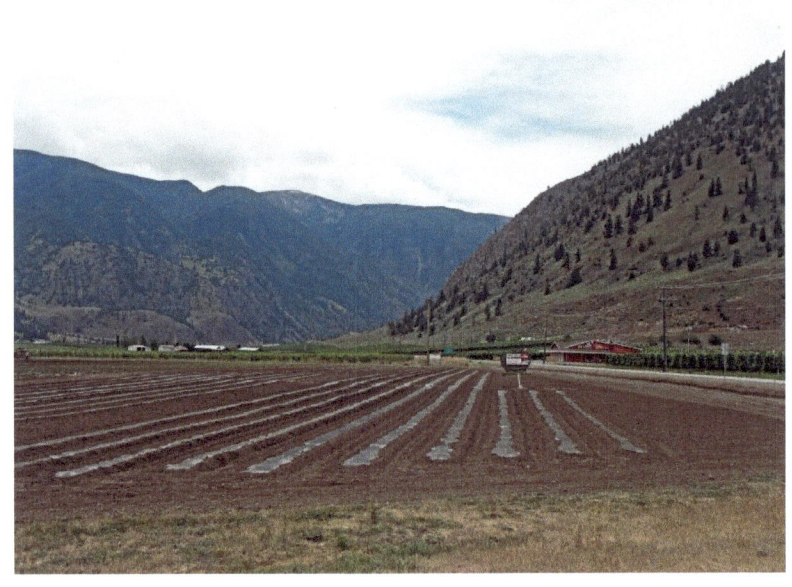

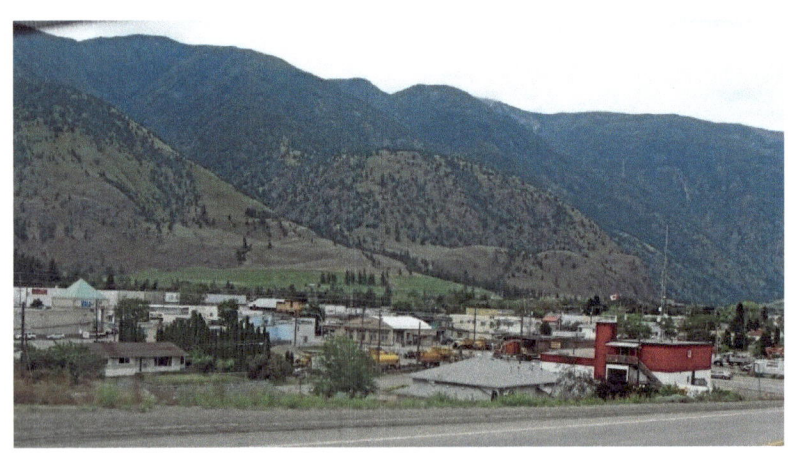

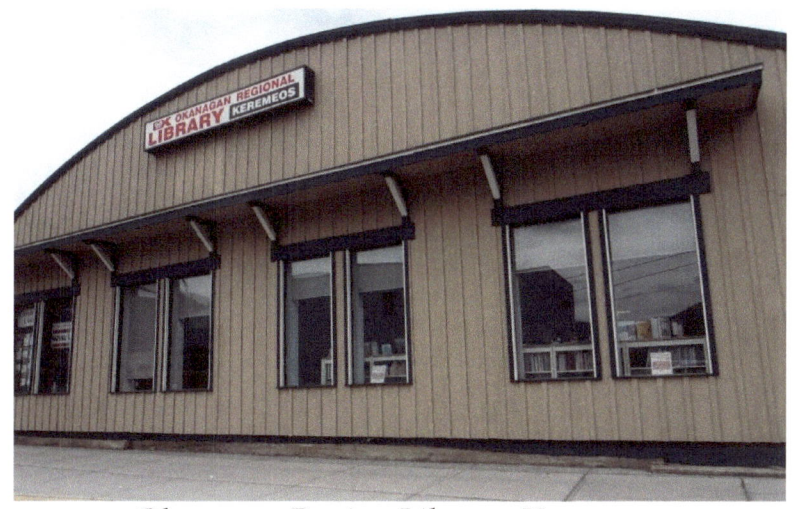

Okanagan Region Library, Keremeos

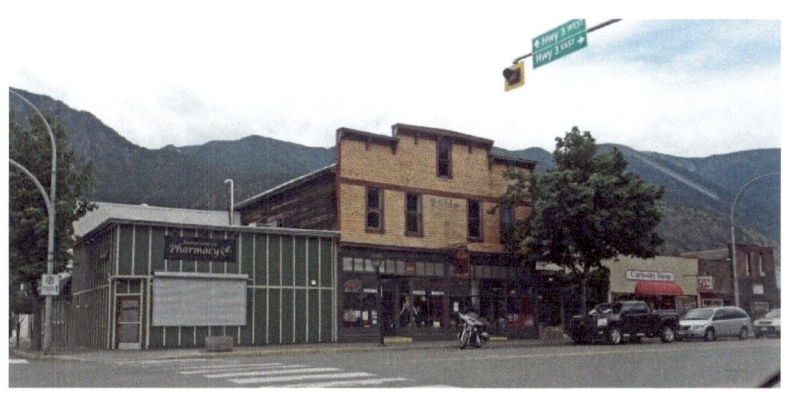

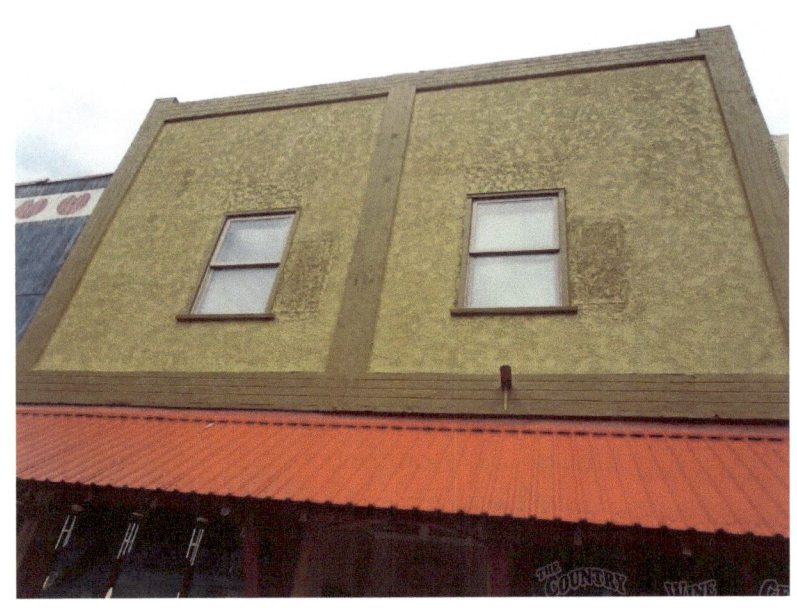

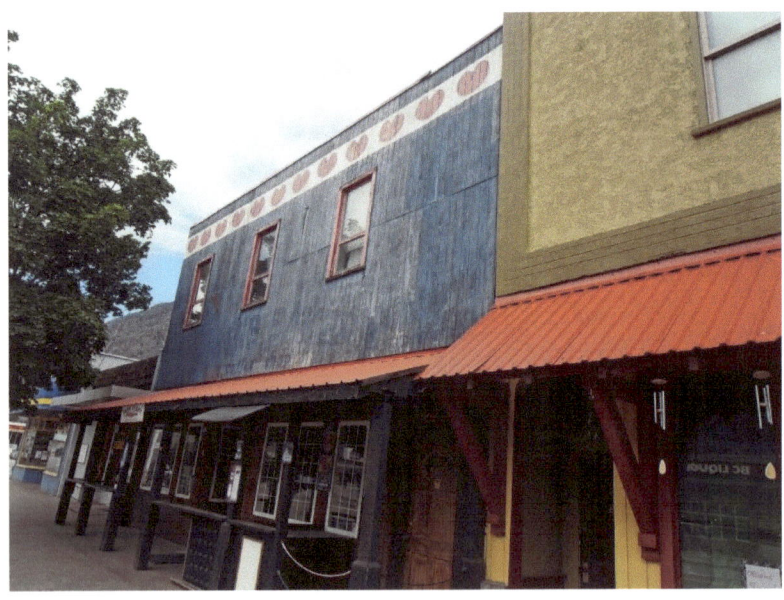

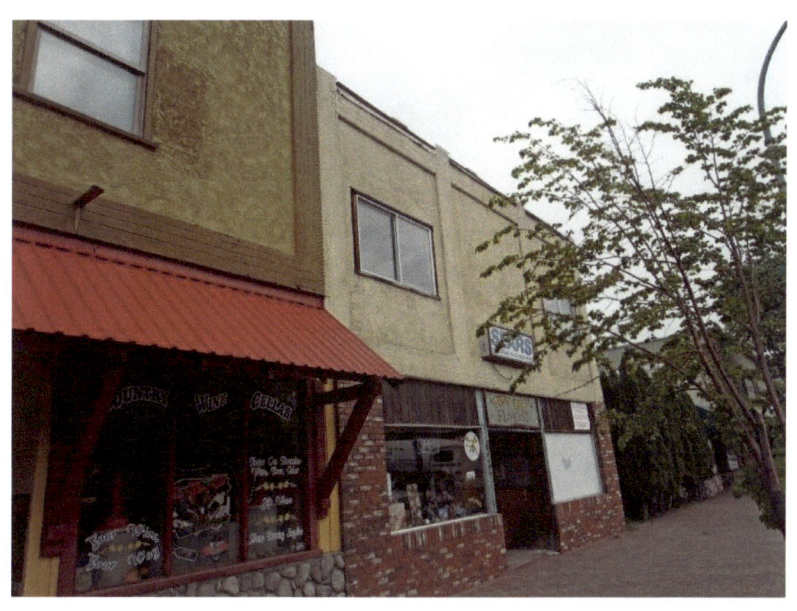

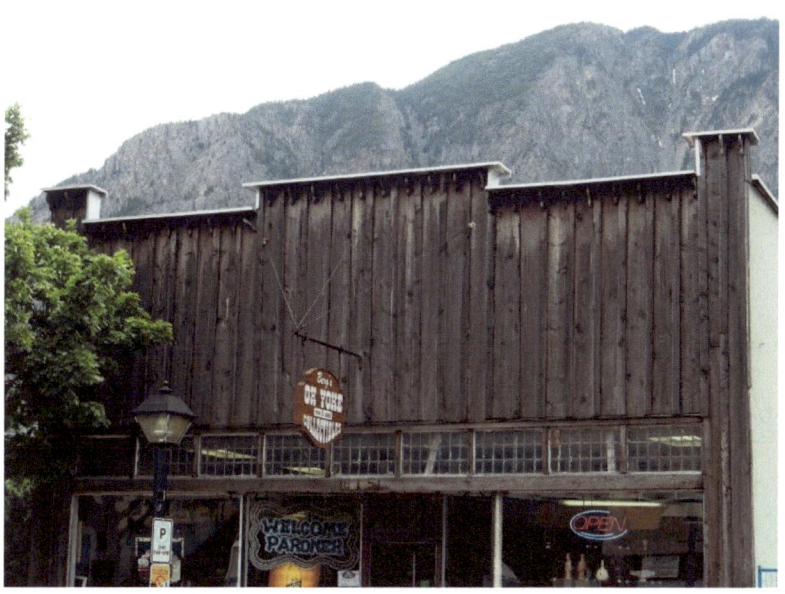

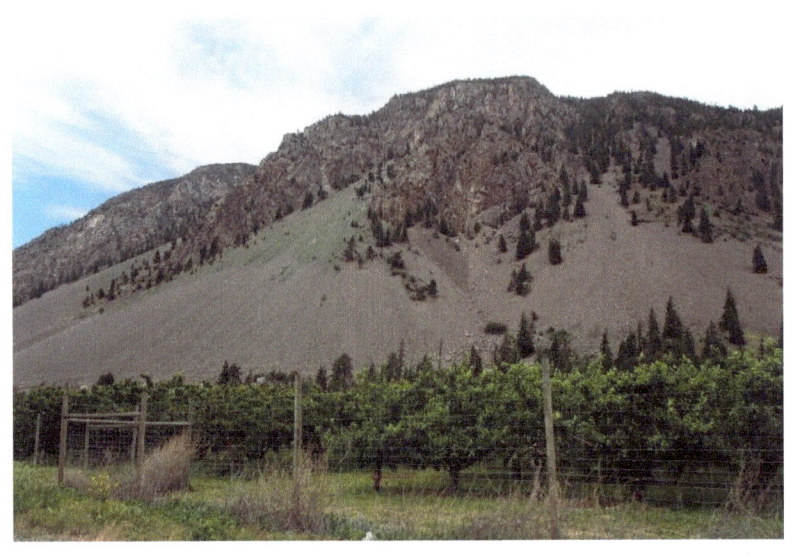

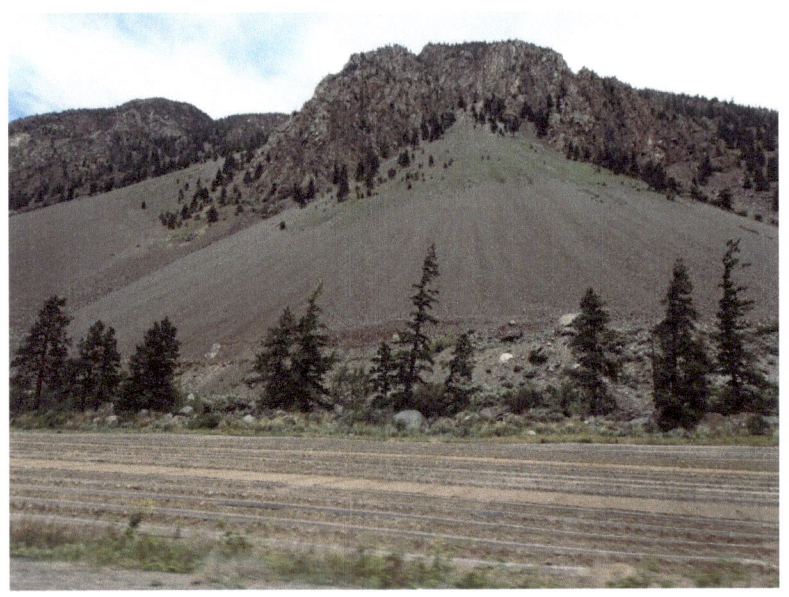

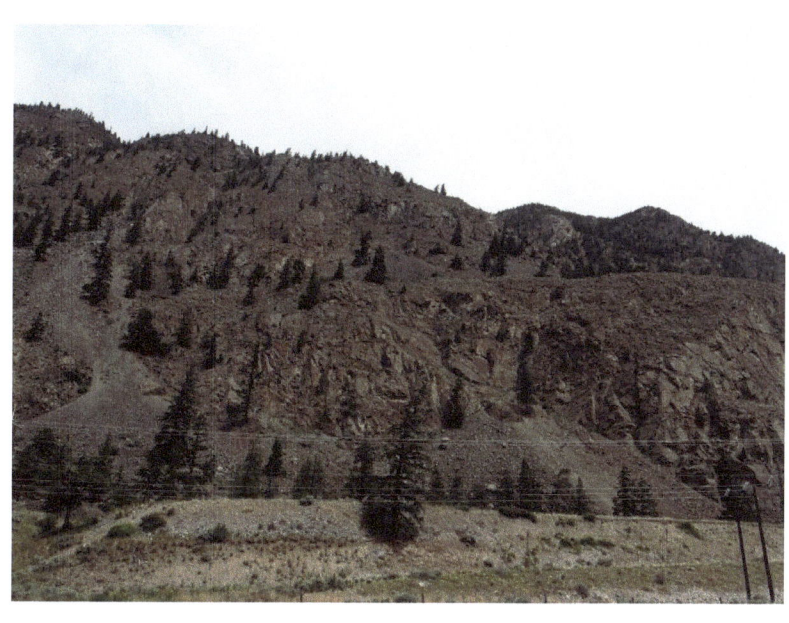

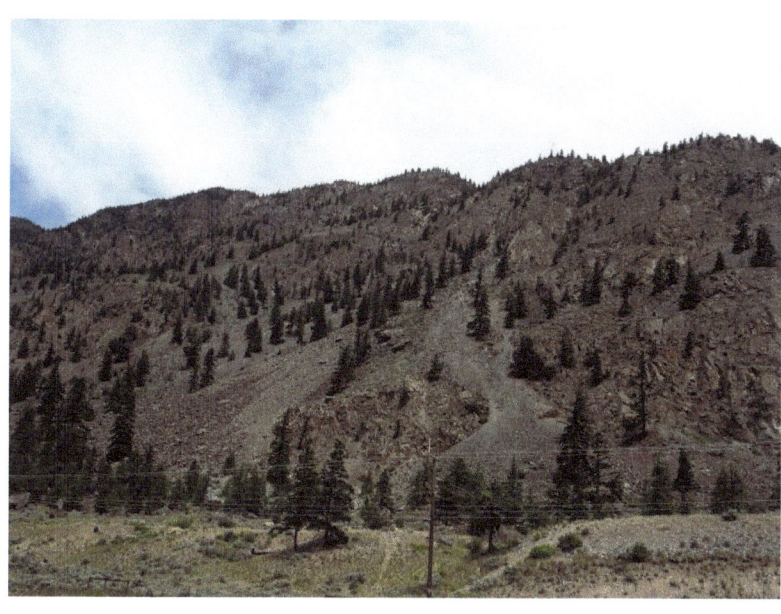

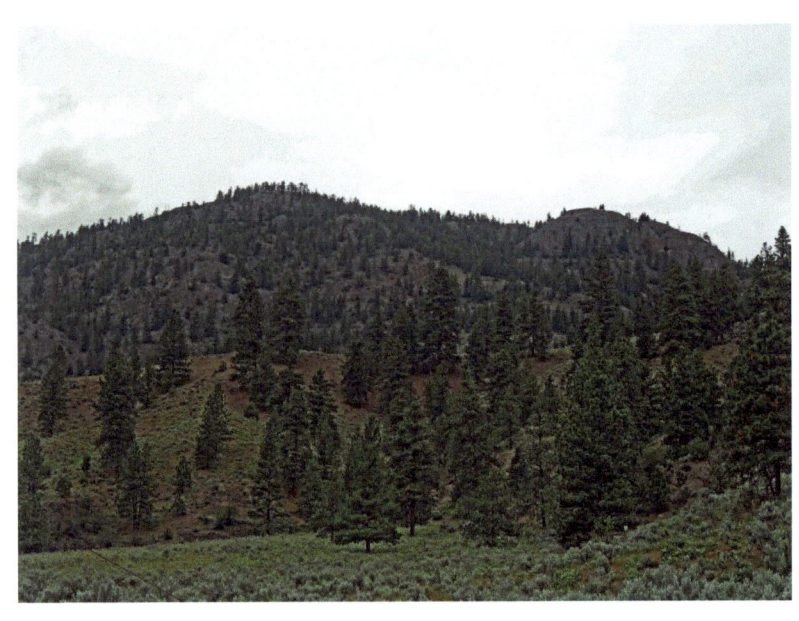

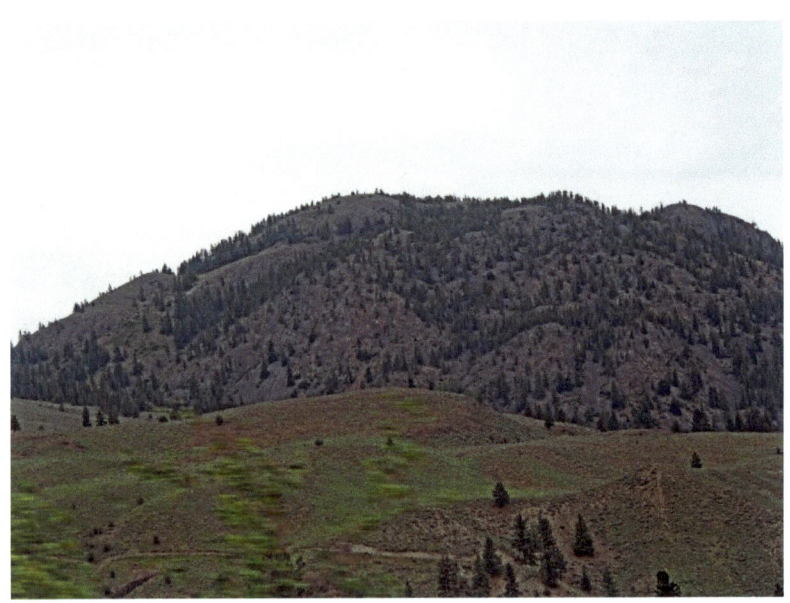

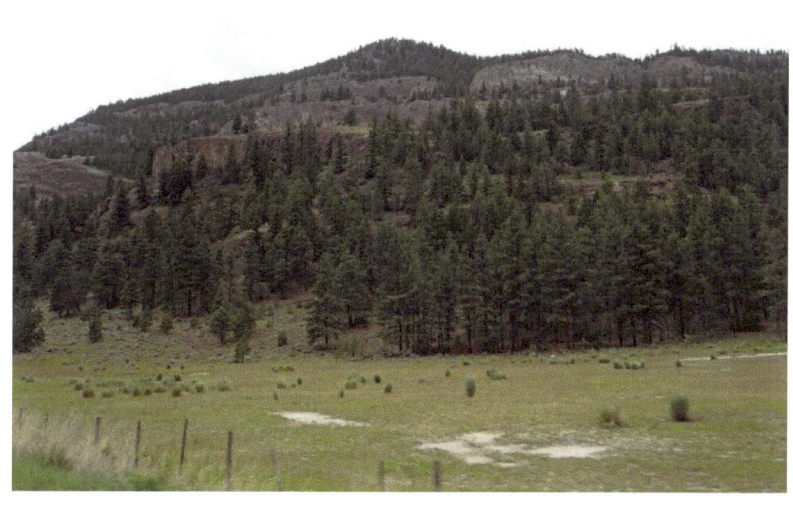

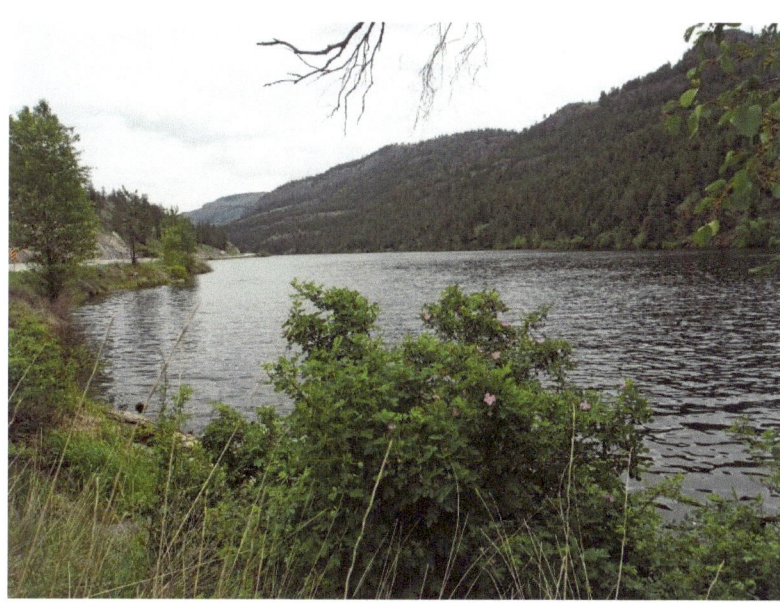

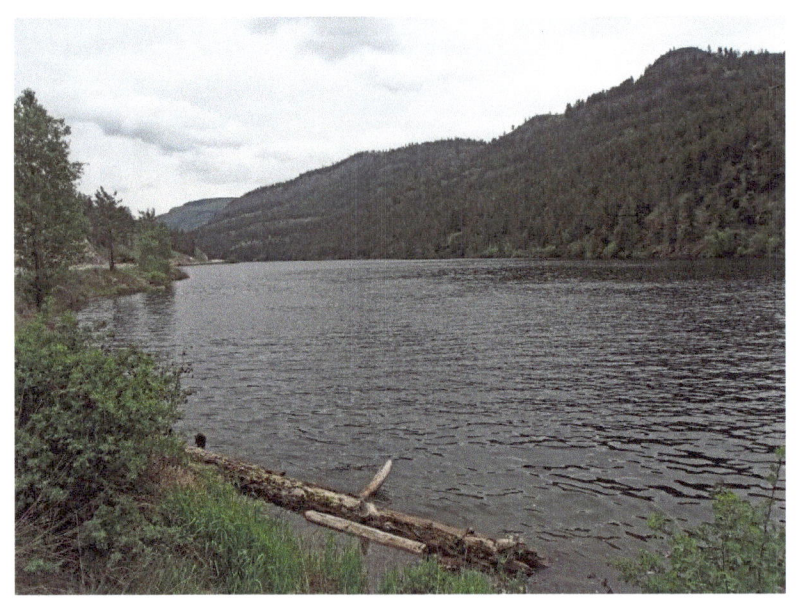

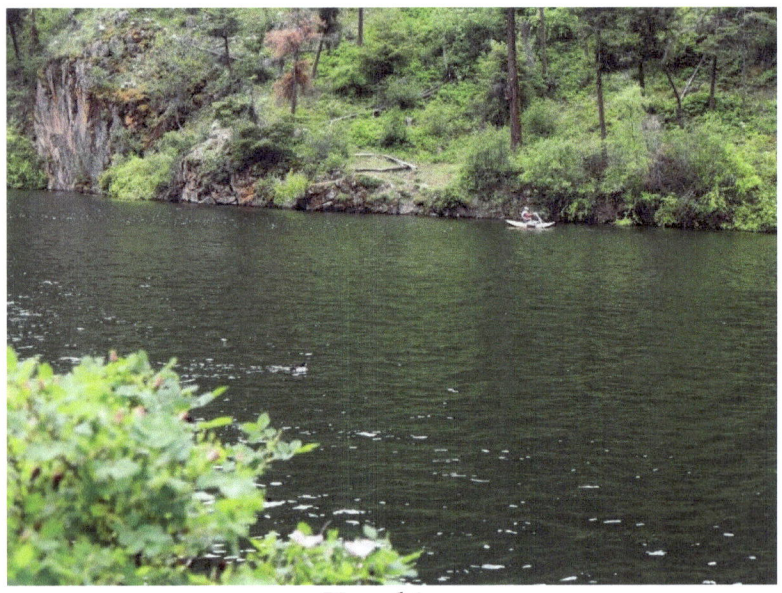

Kayaking

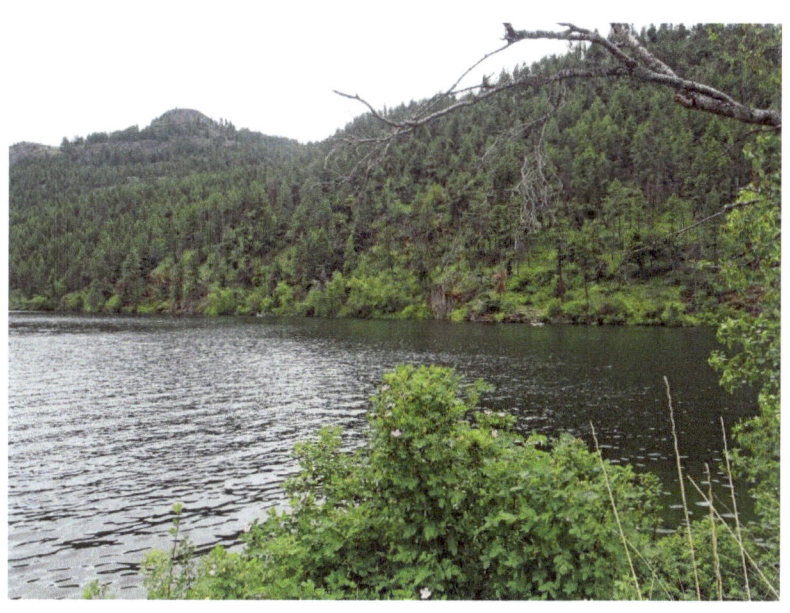

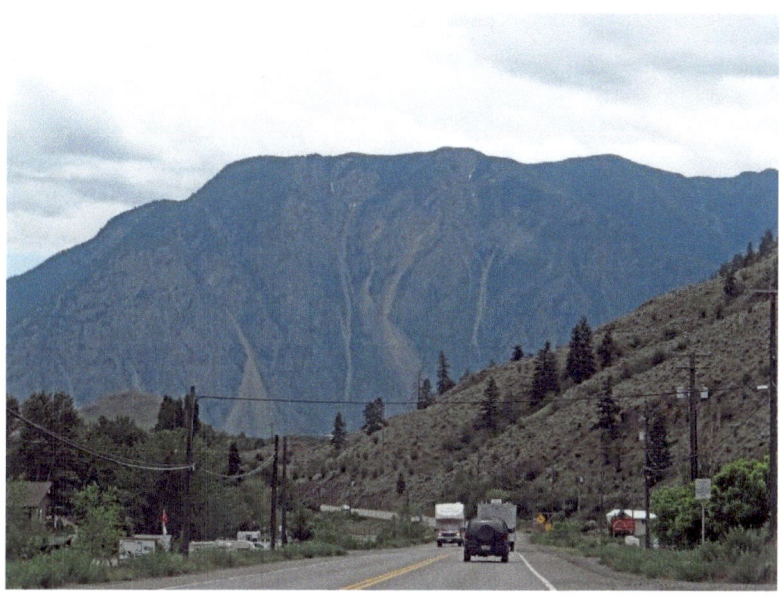

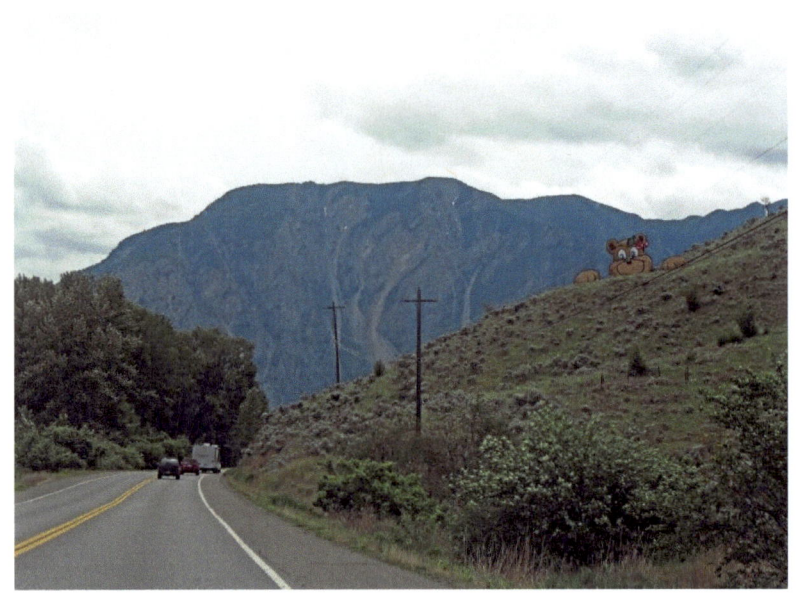

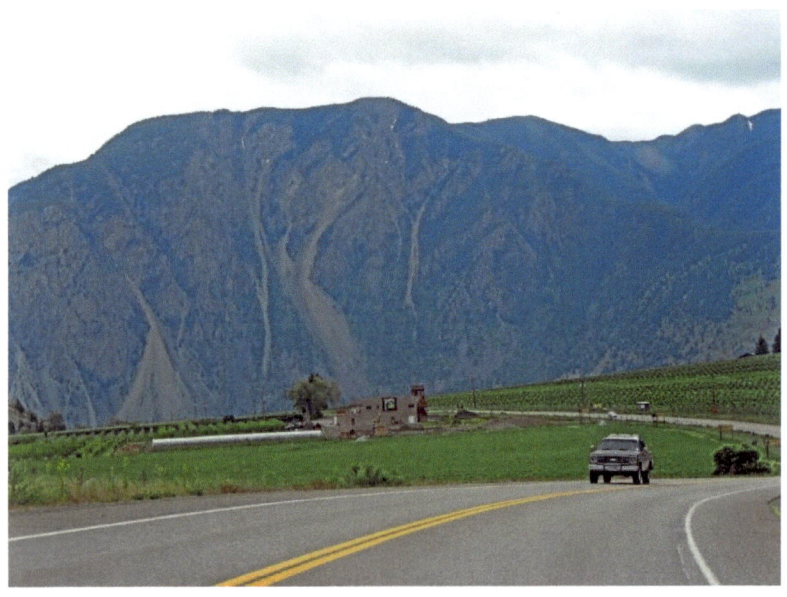

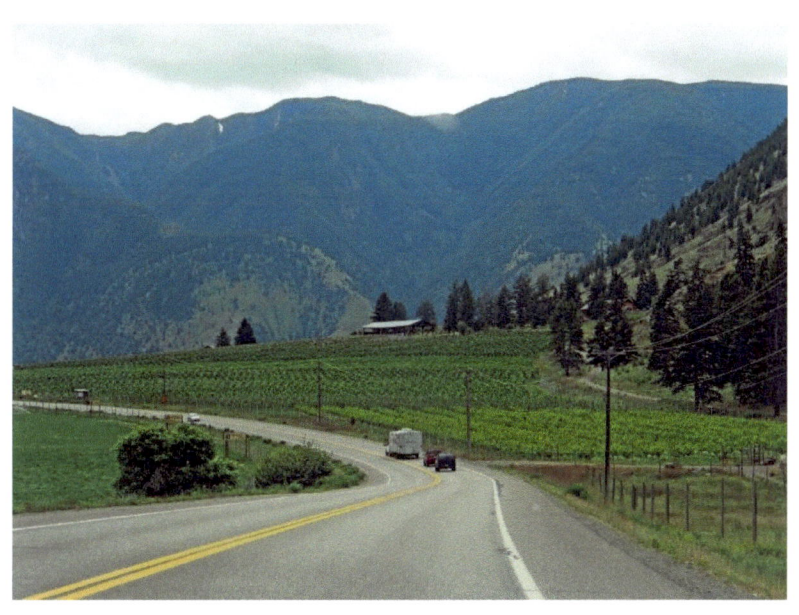

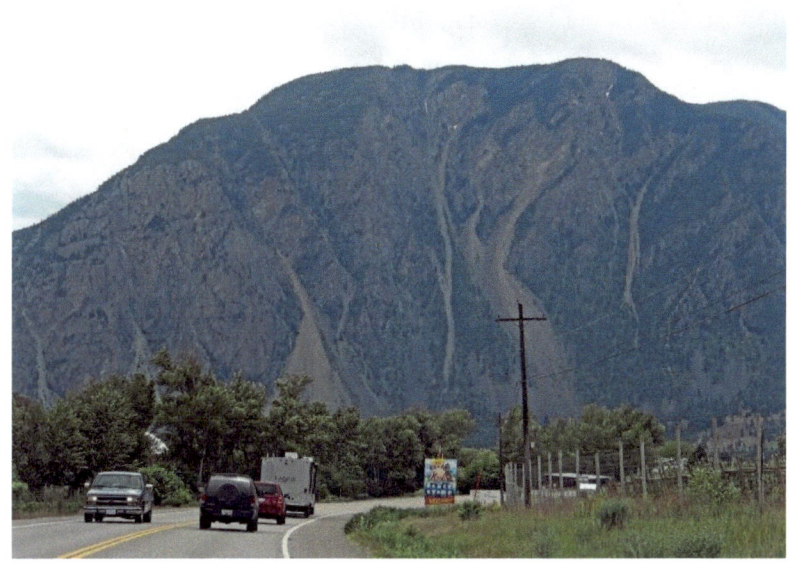

Series Name: Cruising Canada
Saving Our History One Photo at a Time in colour photos

Book 1-9: Winnipeg Manitoba
Book 10: Osoyoos, B.C.
Book 11: Vernon, Salmon Arm
Book 12: Kelowna
Book 13: Penticton
Book 14: Hope

Other Books by Barbara Raue

Coins of Gold
Arrows, Indians and Love
The Life and Times of Barbara
The Cromwell Family Book
Laura Secord Discovered
Daddy Where Are You?

Montana Series
Book 1: Montana Dream
Book 2: Life on the Montana Frontier
Book 3: Montana to Boston and Back
Book 4: Montana Sons Go to War
Book 5: Montana Sons Return From War

Visit Barbara's website to view all of her books
http://barbararaue.ca